Why Must I Suffer?

Why Must I Suffer?

A Book of Light and Consolation

By Rev. F. J. Remler, C.M.

Loreto Publications
2003

Published in 2003 by:
Loreto Publications
P. O. Box 603
Fitzwilliam, NH 03447
www.LoretoPubs.org

Originally published by:
Franciscan Herald Press, 1935

ISBN: 1-930278-29-2

Printed and bound in the United States of America.

Table of Contents

Why Must I Suffer?

Suffering! Is anything more commonly man's lot? Is anything harder to bear? Is there not, even for the most perfect men, one form or another in the range of suffering which would be found a trial? Who then among us but needs consolation? Who but needs at least to be forearmed?

In the following fifteen reasons why God permits suffering, we trust the earnest reader will find light and consolation, which under God's grace will disarm suffering of some of its bitterness, and make a blessing of what is often enough a stumbling block.

One

First Reason:
Sharing the Consequences of Original Sin

Of the many reasons why you must suffer, the first and principal one is this: As a child of Adam and a member of the great human family, you must, like all the rest of men, endure your share of the painful consequence of original sin.

Man's Original Endowments

If there had been no original sin, suffering would be unknown among the children of men. Conditions of life would be entirely different than they are now, for we would be living in that state of marvelous perfection in which Adam was created, a perfection which would exclude every physical and moral evil more effectually than the bright rays of the rising sun banish from the earth the darkness of night.

But in what would this perfection consist? It would consist in the first place in the endowments of what is called Pure Human Nature. By this is meant that we would possess the faculties of our soul – memory, understanding, and free will – the members, organs and senses of our body, in that degree of completeness which would be required to make us what we were designed to be – rational beings – composed of a spiritual soul and an animal body. We would possess, without any defect or deficiency, all the qualities necessary to make us perfect in our order of being: A keen mind, a faithful memory, a strong will, and perfection of bodily form, beauty, health, and vigor. There would be an entire absence of those numerous defects of soul and body which we now labor under because of the deterioration brought on by sin.

In the second place, we would be enriched with the endowments of what is known as the perfection of supernature. At our entrance into the world the gift of supernatural grace would be conferred on us, by which we would be elevated high above the plane of pure nature and adopted by God as His most dear children, with the right and title to the endless enjoyment of the glory of Heaven. After having lived in bliss and happiness on this earth for the length of time decreed by God we would be translated, without tasting the bitterness of death, into "the kingdom prepared for us from the foundation of the world" (Matt. 25:34).

In the third place, this elevation to the state of supernature would include the bestowal of a number of extraordinary endowments which constitute what is called the perfection of preternature. We would possess an extensive knowledge of natural and supernatural truths; we would be free from ignorance and from liability to error in the acquisition of new knowledge; we would also be free from evil concupiscence, because our inclinations and the so-called passions would be so perfectly at the command of the will that they could not become rebellious nor impel us to commit sin. In addition we would possess two very remarkable endowments, the one of impassibility or freedom from every form of suffering, and the other of immortality or freedom from the painful ordeal of death. God created man incorruptible and immortal. Death was not meant for him.

In a word we should all be the happy heirs of that vast assemblage of wonderful gifts which Adam received in his creation and which he possessed up to the moment of his fall from grace.

The Effects of Our Disinheritance

The effects produced by our disinheritance are the following:

First, we were completely stripped of *all the endowments of supernature.* We lost sanctifying grace and with it the sonship of children of God and the right and title to Heaven. No longer well-beloved children of God, we were children of wrath and outcasts from our home in Heaven. Only for the redeeming grace of Jesus Christ, Heaven would have remained closed against us forever.

Second, we also completely lost *all the endowments of preternature* – our freedom from ignorance, concupiscence, sufferings and death. Our intellect has become clouded; our will greatly weakened, and our passions have grown turbulent and rebellious; we suffer much from sickness and disease, from the elements, from accidents and catastrophes, from famines and wars; we must endure the natural results of our own sins and of the sins of others, such as unkindness, hatred, deceit, injustice, oppression, cruelty and the like. And finally, we must undergo the penalty of death. "It is appointed unto men once to die" (Heb. 9:27).

Third, while we did *not incur the loss of the gifts of pure nature,* since these are essential for our existence as human beings, we nevertheless suffered a great deterioration in them. Our natural faculties were much impaired. Our intellect lost its former keenness and wide range of perception; the reason became clouded and liable to every kind of error; the will was so weakened that it became the plaything of the passions, which, like rebellious slaves, usurped the dominion that was formerly exercised by the reason and the will. As a consequence we find that they keep impelling us into the commission of all kinds of sinful excesses.

The final outcome of our disinheritance can be summed up as follows: Left to ourselves and unaided by grace, we tend toward sin as naturally as a stone is drawn to the earth by gravity, as readily as a boat that is caught in a strong current is carried downstream. Sin is a deadly poison to soul and body alike. It invariably produces spiritual and physical deterioration. Of course with the help of grace it is possible to resist the allurements of sin; but as the greater number of men reject this God-given help, vice and crime inevitably abound, directly producing the distressing conditions we witness on every side. In the words of the prophet Osee: "There is no truth, there is no mercy, there is no knowledge of God in the land; cursing and lying and killing and theft and adultery have overflowed, and blood hath touched blood" (Osee 4:1).

Thus were all the evils that afflict mankind introduced into the world by original sin.

An illustration taken from life will serve to make the truth of original sin and its effects more easily understood. Imagine a multimillionaire, the father of a happy family of several children. As long as he administers his affairs carefully, his children have everything they can desire to make them happy. They know nothing of poverty, want, destitution, hunger or starvation. Their needs are looked after, their health is tenderly cared for, and no pains are spared to give them a good education. When their father dies, each one will receive a fixed share of the paternal wealth, in virtue of the right of inheritance.

But the man becomes a drunkard and a reckless gambler. In a short time he loses all he owns, even his house and home – he is a ruined man, reduced to beggary and want, forced to live in the poor house.

However, his criminal conduct involves not only himself, who alone bears the guilt, but also his children, who are entirely innocent of their father's wrongdoing. Once they were happy in the possession of everything apt to make their life pleasant and above all, they held the full right of one day inheriting their father's immense wealth, together with his good name and social prestige; now they are reduced to wretchedness and misery, their hopes of a bright future are rudely shattered, and in place of a large fortune they are doomed to poverty, destitution and other sufferings. Though innocent of any wrongdoing, they are nevertheless affected in a most intimate and painful manner by the inexcusable folly of their father. The law of cause and effect is at work, and it is pitiless in its operation. It makes no allowance for the children's innocence. Though they are in no way implicated in their father's sinful conduct, they must suffer as much as if they, and not he, had been guilty of squandering their fortune.

In much the same way we are now subject to the sad consequences of the loss of our supernatural inheritance in which Adam involved us by his sin of disobedience. We are born into this world in a state of disinheritance, deprived of those wonderful gifts and endowments which were set aside for us from the beginning. Like the unfortunate children of a ruined millionaire, we bear the miseries of life as though we, and not our first parent, were the real transgressors.

This is the first and principal reason why sufferings of every kind come thick and fast into our lives.

"O Happy Sin of Adam!"

But here we must add a reflection that will serve for our consolation in the midst of our trials. Thanks to the infinite wisdom and goodness of God, our present lot, sad though it undoubtedly is, is by no means as hopeless as it would seem to be at first sight. In the light which our holy Faith sheds on this subject, the state of suffering is seen to be a state of great blessedness and of unlimited possibilities to increase our glory in Heaven. Divine Wisdom has contrived in a most wonderful way to draw immense good out of so great an evil. "*O felix culpa* – O happy sin of Adam, which has merited for us so great a Redeemer!" is the jubilant hymn of gratitude and gladness which re-echoes in our churches on Holy Saturday. And why? Because Jesus Christ has made adequate atonement for Adam's sin and now offers us a copious supply of His redeeming and saving grace which more than compensates for the loss of our original inheritance. True, this grace does not restore the Paradise which once existed on earth, nor does it remove from our lives the evils and miseries which spring from original sin; but it does what is infinitely better and more profitable to us in the end – it enables us to endure all sufferings with patience and resignation, to sanctify them by uniting them with the bitter passion and death of Our Lord, converting them into sources of rich supernatural merit, which in turn will procure for us in Heaven a throne far more glorious and exalted than if we had not fallen in Adam from the state of our original perfection.

But it is objected: "If God foreknew the fatal consequences of original sin, why did He not prevent Adam from committing that sin?" or: "Why does God not hinder the commission of sin now?" or again: "Why does He not hinder wicked persons from doing what brings suffering to the innocent?" To these objections the only answer is this: God has created man a free agent. The noblest faculty man possesses is his *free will*. With the exercise of this faculty God does not interfere in any way. Any interference would mean a limitation, a deprivation of free will, at least partially. This would in turn mean that man is not responsible for his moral actions. Interference with his free will would also do away with merit and demerit; reward for good deeds and punishment for evil acts.

Man is left entirely to his own counsel – perfectly free to choose between good and evil, obedience and disobedience, virtue and vice, Heaven and Hell. Whichever he chooses shall be his inheritance. In the lifelong struggle against the forces of evil – the Devil, the world and the flesh, man has at his disposal the powerful aids of Divine grace, by the right use of which he can avoid sin and do good; but God will not in any way *compel* him to use this grace, or to act one way rather than another.

Many abuse this noble faculty by doing what they know is forbidden and sinful, and thereby they become the authors of suffering for themselves and their fellowmen. God does not *will* this, but He *permits* it. In the meantime, His infinite wisdom and fatherly providence direct even the sinful actions of men to the furtherance of the welfare and salvation of His elect, even as He turned the malice and enmity of the Jews against Our Lord to the accomplishment of the redemption of man from sin and Hell.

Two

Second Reason:
Expiation of Public and National Sins

The second reason why you must suffer, especially in times of general calamity, is this: As a member of society and a citizen of your country, you must unite with the rest in making the atonement and reparation which Divine Justice requires for the public and national sins committed in the community in which you live.

By public and national sins we understand certain sins of a graver nature which are committed on so large a scale and by so many persons in a community, be it a city, or a province, or an entire nation, that they are attributed to the community as a body and not merely to this or that individual. Sins of this kind are: Apostasy from the Faith, irreligion and forgetfulness of God; godless education of the young; profanation of God's Holy Name, cursing, blasphemy and perjury; the desecration of the Lord's Day; immodest and scandalous fashions; immoral art, literature and amusements; divorce and adultery sanctioned by iniquitous state laws; dishonesty, injustice and oppression of the poor; murder and race suicide; and finally, those wild orgies of gross immorality and unrestrained license which periodically disgrace public festivities and celebrations, or occur in connection with balls, dances, banquets and the like.

God is exceedingly patient and long-suffering, and does not willingly inflict general chastisements, however richly they may be deserved by a community. He rather desires that His offending children seek His pardon by means of a timely repentance and conversion. He waited a hundred years before He sent the deluge which He had commissioned Noe to announce; He allowed forty years to elapse between the prediction made by Our Lord of the coming destruction of Jerusalem and the fulfillment of that prediction by the Romans in the year 70; and He spared the city of Ninive altogether because its inhabitants immediately left off sinning and hastened to do penance at the preaching of Jonas.

God acts in this way still. He often waits a long time before He inflicts on sinful cities and nations those more extensive chastisements which their multiplied iniquities call for. He desires to spare them and therefore tries first in every possible way to recall them to a sense of their duty and to timely repentance and conversion. But if in spite of these delays they obstinately refuse to enter into themselves and to leave off sinning; if they continue in their wickedness, sometimes even to the extent of sinning more boldly because their evil deeds are not punished at once, then the hour must come in which the measure of their iniquity is filled to overflowing. That hour will mark the beginning of some general visitation which will fall heavily on the guilty community as a just punishment of its long continued transgressions of God's Holy Law – destructive floods or storms, conflagrations, earthquakes; seasons of scarcity and famine; epidemics and pestilences; and especially the horrors of rebellions and revolutions, and of civil and international wars. Divine Justice makes use of these evils for the punishment and correction of a sinful people much the same as a wise father uses the rod for the chastisement and betterment of a wayward child.

Nor is it always necessary that God *send* such chastisement for public sins, as He sent the deluge or the destruction of Jerusalem. There are many sins which contain in themselves the seeds of future public suffering just as the acorn contains the gigantic oak. If such sins prevail for a sufficiently long time, unchecked and unrepented, they are bound to produce such conditions in the social order as make certain calamities unavoidable. Take, for example, the sin of *godless* education, that is, education of youth without religion. Where such a system has been adopted, the necessary results must be the following: After two or three generations the knowledge of God will disappear more or less completely among the people; the sense of right and wrong will be lost; good will be called evil, and evil good; there will be no respect for the moral law; the depravity of youth will grow worse and worse; dishonesty and corruption will prevail in business, in the courts, in the legislature, and in the government itself; taxes will be misappropriated or disappear in the pockets of grafters; heavy expenses will be necessary to maintain the growing number of asylums, juvenile courts, reform schools and prisons; there will be no security to honor property and life; the relations between capital and labor will be strained to the breaking point, so that violence and bloodshed will become inevitable; family life will be disrupted by adultery, divorce and free love; national rivalries, jealousies and hatreds, provoked by commercial greed, grow more and more intense, until they lead to international wars with their unspeakable misery to millions. Nations that sow the whirlwind must reap the storm.

Public and national sins must be expiated in this world for the very simple reason that they cannot be expiated in the next. In the world to come families, cities, provinces and nations will have no continued corporate existence. There, men and women will exist merely as individuals, without being united by those social, civil, political and national bonds which are necessary in this life for the welfare and preservation of the human race. In eternity, they will individually enjoy the fruits of their life on earth – the good will possess the kingdom of God in Heaven, while the wicked shall suffer for their evil deeds in the unquenchable fire of Hell. But as public sins require public expiation, and as this expiation cannot be made in this next life, it is clear that it must be made on this side of the grave.

Why Must the Innocent Suffer?

A question which proves a sore temptation to many persons whose faith is weak and unenlightened suggests itself in this connection: Why is it that the good and virtuous are not exempt at such times, but are compelled to suffer like the rest? If God is just, how can He allow the innocent to be afflicted with the guilty?

There are several reasons why God permits the good to suffer in times of public chastisement:

1. It is but right and just that the good should lend a willing hand in offering to God the atonement made necessary by public sins, because in normal times they enjoy in common with their fellow-citizens the blessings of peace, tranquillity, national prosperity. Their temporal interests are common, both in times of prosperity and in times of affliction.

2. Those who are innocent of actually taking part in public sins are not for that reason always wholly free from guilt in the sight of God. Very often they are guilty of these sins in an indirect manner — accessory to them, as it is called. Thus they may have connived at some form of immorality; they may not have protested against it; they may have neglected to use their authority, or influence, or right to vote, to hinder its introduction, or to procure its removal when already introduced, and all this from indifference, human respect, fear of persecution, of loss of business and similar unworthy reasons.

3. The sufferings endured by the good have a much greater atoning value than those endured by the wicked. Hence the more good persons there are to join in making the required atonement, the more quickly will it be made. Besides, God is easily moved, out of consideration for the sufferings of the good, greatly to mitigate His punishments, and sometimes even to cancel them altogether.

4. The sight of the good suffering for sins which they did not commit is apt to promote the conversion and salvation of the wicked, by vividly reminding them of the more rigorous chastisements inflicted for sin in the next life. If sin is punished so severely upon the good here on earth, how much more severely will it be punished upon unrepentant sinners in eternity!

5. Such sufferings afford the good an opportunity of making full atonement for their personal sins. For there is no one so holy and so confirmed in grace that he has not committed some sins, such at least as are venial. "Even the just man shall fall seven times," i.e., frequently. But it is an unchanging law that every sin, even the smallest, must be fully expiated either here, or hereafter in Purgatory. But expiation made here is vastly more profitable than that which is made after death.

6. The patient endurance of undeserved suffering makes the good resemble Jesus Christ, who, though perfectly innocent, took upon Himself the task of making atonement for our sins and thereby opening Heaven to us. If He had not made this atonement, we could not be saved. Besides, innocent sufferings enable the good to reach the highest degrees of grace and virtue here, which will produce for them a correspondingly high degree of endless glory in the kingdom of Heaven.

Three

Third Reason:
Natural Results of Indiscretions

In vindication of God's goodness and love and of His dealings with men, it must be said with clearness and emphasis, that He is by no means to be held responsible for all the evil there is in the world. A very large amount of human suffering is not at all of God's sending, but entirely of man's own making.

We do not hesitate to assert that probably half, if not more, of present-day miseries would quickly disappear from the face of the earth if people could be universally induced to fulfill faithfully just two conditions, and they are, that they live according to the dictates of right reason and common sense, observing the fundamental laws of health and well-being, and that they make an honest effort to shape their moral conduct according to the Ten Commandments and the maxims of the Gospel.

In this chapter we will consider the first of these two points and study how sins against right reason, as we shall call them, are the direct and necessary cause of much unnecessary suffering. Of sins against the Commandments as necessary causes of suffering we shall treat in the next chapter.

Sickness and Disease

No one can question the evident truth that our life, health and temporal happiness are controlled by well-defined laws, which cannot be changed or abolished by the will of man. They can indeed be disregarded and violated, but never with impunity. Their observance is generally rewarded with the enjoyment of health and freedom from many forms of sickness and other evils; while no man can violate these laws with impunity, any more than he can hold his hand in the fire and sustain no injury. In fact, so close and necessary is the connection between cause and effect, that nothing but a miracle can save a man from the consequences of violating one of these laws. Let us give a few examples by way of illustration.

There are people who in their advanced years are sorely tried by chronic ailments which make their life a prolonged misery. Can it be true that in every case these ailments were sent by God? By no means. Very often they are the necessary results of the indiscretions which these persons committed times without number in their younger days. The stern laws of health were violated, and here is the punishment. People who recklessly expose themselves to the inclemency of the weather; who have the injurious habit of eating in a hurry and of not taking the time to masticate their food properly; who neglect to take a sufficient amount of outdoor exercise; who habitually breathe incorrectly; who indulge immoderately in malnutritious delicacies to the exclusion of plain but wholesome and nutritious food; women who by the foolish use of tight or otherwise incorrect apparel inflict permanent injury on certain members and organs whose proper functioning is indispensable for good health - these people in later life pay dearly for the sins against good sense which they committed by violating the unchangeable laws which control life and health. Outraged nature knows no mercy and grants no pardon. Sooner or later she wreaks terrible vengeance, exacting full payment of the penalty.

These ills must therefore be considered as being not of God's sending but of man's own making.

Others there are who are afflicted with painful diseases of the heart, stomach, liver, kidneys, or other organs, which render them invalids for life. Does God always send these diseases? No. Very often they are only the necessary results of irrational and intemperate living, of gluttony, or long continued indulgence in alcoholic drinks, or in opiates, or other injurious drugs – self-caused ailments, for which God must not be blamed. Habits of life regulated by common sense, self-control, and the cardinal virtue of temperance could have been rewarded with freedom from these painful afflictions.

Then again there are many victims of what is called a nervous breakdown. What is the cause? In very many cases it is a mode of life which tramples under foot every known law of health. During the day, the victims are shut up in close, stuffy, unsanitary shops, mills, factories, stores or offices; their meals are usually taken in a hurry; they consist mostly of articles that merely stimulate or gratify the taste, but do not nourish the body, being void of those elements which are necessary to repair wasted tissue, to build up new tissue, and to produce the required heat of the body. Many of the products sold in our confectioneries, drug stores, and refreshment parlors have very little nutritive value, not to mention the fact that they are often adulterated by unscrupulous makers and dealers, who are more interested in making big profits than in maintaining the health of their patrons. As well might we try to keep up a good fire with low grade coal as try to keep up health and vigor with food that lacks the elements necessary for proper nutrition.

But this is not all. Frequently a weakened constitution is still more taxed by spending the greater part of the night in exhausting and nerve-racking excitement, at theaters, parties, socials, dances and the like, thus depriving it of the sleep and rest essential to good health. And finally, there is often enough reckless indulgence in sins of impurity, which by themselves and apart from all other causes are destructive to the nervous system and often ruin it beyond the hope of repair.

Can it be a surprise, then, if after several years of such irrational living there comes at last a collapse from which there is no recovery? The surprise would be if it did not come. Only a miracle can avert it. That nervous breakdown with its attendant misery, let it be well understood, is not of God's sending, but often as not the necessary result of indiscretions – it is of the sufferer's own making.

Domestic Troubles

Let us consider another class of sufferings. There are those who have no end of domestic troubles. But why? Often because they are reaping the harvest of past folly. "What a man sows, that also shall he reap." They may have married thoughtlessly and at sight, without sufficient deliberation and in open violation of the laws of God and of the Church, and therefore without the blessing of Heaven. Instead of preparing for marriage by prayer, the reception of the sacraments and a virtuous life, they gave themselves up to sinful indulgence, and God's displeasure followed them into their newly established home. The young man married a woman of whom he knew that she was a flighty creature, giddy and vain, without character, unable or unwilling to attend to household duties, extravagant, a slave of fashion, unwilling to bring up children, not ready for any sacrifice. He married her face, as the saying is, or her money, or social standing. Now he must put up with the results of his foolish choice. Or, the young woman gave her affections to a man who she knew to be unsteady in his habits, unreliable, dishonest and lazy, unable to hold a position, addicted to drink or to drugs, who did not respect her virtue during their courtship, and even at that time showed signs of future infidelity. Though aware of all this and often warned of her danger, she took no heed, but in her infatuation for him flattered herself that she would convert him. Now she is painfully undeceived, but it is too late. She is condemned to repent at leisure.

Or, it is a mixed marriage. The Catholic wife suffers much from her non-Catholic relatives, who ridicule her Church and her Faith; her husband makes life miserable for her by compelling her to do things which her conscience tells her are mortally sinful before God; or, she has the sorrow of seeing her children one by one give up the religion of their childhood to imitate the easy-going ways of the non-Catholic father.

Is it any wonder that in such homes there are frequent bickerings, quarrels, family scenes, desertions, leading up to the disgraceful proceedings of the divorce court, perhaps even to cruel murder? And will anyone have the hardihood to assert that sufferings springing from causes of this kind are sent by God? Thoughtfulness before marriage, a life of prayer and observance of the Commandments, and a faithful compliance with the wise laws by which the Church regulates the marriages of her children, would, we do not hesitate to affirm, do away with perhaps nine-tenths of the unhappy marriages that we meet with in these days of reckless disregard for the holiness of matrimony.

Then again there are parents who suffer much from their grown children, who are unruly and wayward, and bring disgrace on their family by immorality and crime. Very commonly this is the natural outcome of a perverted or neglected education. Perhaps the parents gave their sons and daughters no religious training; they neglected to instill the knowledge, fear and love of God into their minds and hearts. Or, if they sent them to a Catholic school, they failed to set them a good example at home, thus neutralizing the efforts of pastors and teachers to make them God fearing boys and girls. Then, there are parents who are over-indulgent toward their children, allowing them their way in everything, wilfully blind to their failings, not correcting, much less punishing them, even when they commit serious faults. They "spare the rod and spoil the child." The day comes when their petted and spoiled sons and daughters are the cause of great grief and sorrow to them by their ingratitude, neglect, ill-treatment, even cruelty, or through the shame and disgrace which they bring upon their families. "Bow down his (thy son's) neck while he is young, and beat his sides while he is a child, lest he grow stubborn and regard thee not, and so be a sorrow of heart to thee" (Eccles. 30:12).

When such fathers and mothers find their old age full of grief and sorrow caused by wayward sons and daughters, who is responsible? Surely they must not put the blame upon Almighty God. They themselves are the authors of their unhappiness. If they had trained their children along the lines traced by right reason, common sense and the light of Faith, they would have found in their children a support in their old age and an unfailing source of happiness in their declining years. As it is, they are reaping the natural fruits for their past folly.

Other Troubles

Finally, there are many who for their indiscretions are reduced to great poverty. Either they did not practice thrift and economy in the management of their domestic affairs; or they were discontented with their humble station and tried to appear more wealthy than their neighbors; or their great ambition was to move in society. Living above their means made it necessary for them to contract large debts which they could not pay; a foreclosure of mortgages followed, and their ruin was complete. Sufferings, again, not God-sent but man-made.

These are but a few of the many examples that could be cited in support of our statement that sins against right reason and common sense are directly responsible for a large percentage of human sufferings, for which it would not be fair to blame God as the author.

Four

Fourth Reason:
Natural Results of Sins Against
the Ten Commandments

If sins against right reason are productive of much suffering, sins against the Ten Commandments are still more so. It is no exaggeration to say that violation of the Commandments is directly responsible for the greatest portion of the misery that scourges the human race. In proof of this let us single out just a few sins, which, as experience and observation show, are a common and fruitful source of much self-inflicted suffering.

Nothing has worked so much detriment to the health of mankind for many centuries as the habits that may be generalized under the term of impurity. "The ravages of venereal diseases have increased just in proportion to the gradual diminution of the influence of religion during the past few generations" (James J. Walsh, *Health and Religion*, p. 185). In countless slaves to the vice of impurity the words of Sacred Scripture are literally verified: "He that sinneth in the sight of his Maker, shall fall into the hands of the physician" (Eccles. 38:15). "If thou give to thy soul her desires, she will make thee a joy to thy enemies" (Eccles. 18:31). "He that joineth himself to harlots, will be wicked; rottenness and worms shall inherit him" (Eccles. 19:3). "His bones shall be filled with the vices of his youth, and they shall sleep with him in the dust" (Job 20:11). The life of many a man and woman is embittered by a disease so loathsome that it makes its victims a grievous torment to themselves and to their surroundings, and often tempts them to seek relief from their misery in suicide. But how did they contract it? Very commonly by sinful indulgence of the passion of lust, either on their part or on the part of those with whom they are associated. A life of purity and chastity would have preserved them from the ravages of this dreadful scourge.

To understand how much misery is caused by the vice of impurity, we need only visit some general hospital or asylum. Persons of every age and rank, young and old, rich and poor, are there reaping the harvest of iniquity and sin. Decay of the body, and often, too, of the mind, is apparent in their wretched forms. They are dying a living death. How dearly they are paying for having tasted the poison cup of forbidden pleasures! And what an unequal bargain they struck! For a few brief and fleeting moments of sensual delight they are enduring the ravages of a disease which causes them unceasing pain and defies the skill of the best physicians.

But it is not in hospitals and asylums only that we see the havoc impurity creates among its slaves. There are many persons living in their homes, both in stately mansions and lowly hovels, who must pay dearly for their sinful excesses. Some are suffering from painful disorders which are directly traceable to their past sins; while others are punished in their children, who are afflicted in mind or body. The lot of these innocent victims is pitiable in the extreme. Who bears the blame? In a large number of cases, none other than their parents. By indulgence in unlawful pleasures before or after marriage they became infected with the virulent poison, which they in turn transmitted to their unfortunate offspring.

It was a very natural process, a blind working out of the stern law of cause and effect. Had the parents lived in the fear of God and kept His law, their marital happiness would have been assured; but having trampled on the law, the consequences of their sin involve not only them but also their posterity down to the third and fourth generation. There was no need on the part of God to *send* them a special punishment. These afflictions are so intimately bound up with certain forms of sin, and so necessarily promoted by them, that nothing but a miraculous interference with the laws of nature could save the transgressors from the penalty of their immoral actions. "Not only is death a consequence of these diseases, but they are also frequent causes of long years of suffering and crippling, of the blinding of children and the birth of dead or idiotic children, or of little ones who grow up to be epileptic or to become insane in early adult life, or to exhibit other sad marks of the diseases of their parent." (Idem, p. 186).

The same is true of the victims of alcoholism or of the drug habit. They are guilty of a species of suicide. They wreck their manhood, degrade their reason, and bring on themselves all kinds of domestic trouble, poverty, disease and an untimely death. In addition to this they are usually guilty of grave injustice to their offspring, to whom they transmit their evil propensities, or bequeath bodily or mental infirmities. Great indeed is the number of those persons who owe their defects of mind and body to the fact that the one or the other of their parents was a slave to alcoholism or to the drug habit.

Finally, to take a case which occurs with increasing frequency in these days of neo-pagan ideals in regard to the duties of the married state: A surprisingly large number of women is suffering from no other cause than cold-blooded interference with the order established by God for the procreation of human life. Extremely painful diseases, such as cancer, blood poison, serious mental or nervous disorders which sometimes end in insanity, are making their life a prolonged agony. Once they may have gloried in it that they succeeded in frustrating God's will and designs; they may have rejoiced over the fact that they escaped the burden of bringing up children; they may have succeeded in quieting the reproaches of their conscience by adopting the pagan maxims of the modern world which pronounces even the grossest forms of immorality something innocent and harmless; but there is one thing they could not succeed in doing, and that is to abrogate or change the immutable law of God, the law of nature. They were free to violate the law by committing sins which cry to Heaven for vengeance; but they were not free to escape the natural penalties of these sins. Outraged nature knows no pity and grants no pardon. Their present painful lot is purely the wages of sin – not of God's sending, therefore, but entirely their own making.

Converting Evil Into Good

We have seen how people bring upon themselves much suffering through failure to live according to the laws of good sense and to keep the Ten Commandments. Now the question arises: Is it possible to derive any advantages from such self-caused and self-inflicted sufferings, or is there nothing to do but to resign oneself to the inevitable and stoically put up with the results of one's folly, much the same as a pagan or a fatalist might do, who claims that blind chance controls all human affairs? To this we must answer: As in His infinite wisdom and goodness God contrived to turn Adam's sin into a source of immense spiritual blessing to the world through the life and sufferings of Jesus Christ, so has He made it possible for us to convert all our afflictions – not only those which are unavoidable, but also those which are self-inflicted – into a source of everlasting benefit.

It remains for you, therefore, dear reader, in case you are a victim of sufferings which you have brought on yourself in any way, to learn the secret of turning these to good account. It is true, it was not God's will that you should be thus afflicted. But now that you have failed and brought this evil on yourself, it is God's will that you derive from it all the good that He has made it possible for you to obtain. For this purpose carefully attend to the following important conditions:

1. Imitate the Prodigal Son and return to God with sincere sorrow for your sins, securing the fulness of His pardon by a contrite confession. You must be in the state of grace before your suffering can be meritorious for Heaven.

2. Humbly acknowledge that you have fully deserved your sufferings – nay, even the eternal pains of Hell – by mortal sin. If you have not been condemned, it is solely because God's mercy has spared you and given you time for repentance.

3. In the spirit of an abiding sorrow for your sins, make sure to unite all your sufferings with those of Our Lord dying on the cross, and make a frequent offering of them thus united, to the Divine Justice in atonement for the wrong you have done.

By acting in conformity with these suggestions you will reap a threefold benefit: You will insure the complete pardon of all your sins; you will quickly cancel the debt of temporal punishment contracted by them and thus shorten your Purgatory hereafter; your penitent dispositions will win for you a much higher place in Heaven than you might obtain if you had never fallen into serious sins of any kind.

If therefore you are suffering from self-inflicted sickness, poverty, domestic troubles and the like, do not fail to sanctify them and to beg God to accept them in payment of the temporal punishment due to your sins. Or, if there is anyone in your family, a child or other relative, who needs your constant care and attention, know that this affords you an excellent opportunity for practicing the most perfect kind of Christ-like charity. Lavish upon the sufferer all the kindness you can command, for it is not so much to him that you are ministering as to Our Lord Himself. Never lose sight of His words in this connection: "Amen, I say to you, as long as you did it to one of these my least brethren, you did it to me" (Matt. 25:40).

See then how mercifully God has contrived to make it possible for you to derive endless benefits from your folly.

Five

Fifth Reason:
Temporal Punishment of Your Sins

The fifth reason why you are made to suffer is this: You have committed many sins, and thereby contracted a large debt of temporal punishment. You must cancel this debt either here or hereafter – here, by performing voluntary works of penance or by bearing the sufferings which God sends or allows to come to you; hereafter, by enduring the pains of Purgatory.

We have seen that very much of the misery that men suffer is self-caused and self-inflicted. But after making due allowance for such misery, there are a great many sufferings the causes of which are beyond the control of man. From these there is no escape, any more than there is from death itself. Of this kind are unavoidable accidents and catastrophes, contagious diseases and epidemics, storms, earthquakes and wars, as also those sufferings which have their source in selfishness, unkindness, enmity, injustice and cruelty experienced in our dealings with our fellowmen. What about these sufferings?

Of many, if not all of them, we can rightly say they are sent, or at least permitted, for temporal punishment of our sins. To make this point clear, we must say a few words about the nature of the punishment contracted by sin. Every sin, even the smallest, involves us in two things, *guilt* and *punishment.* By the guilt we understand the offense or insult against God that is contained in a sinful act; and by the punishment we mean the atonement or reparation that must be made for it. This punishment is twofold, *eternal* and *temporal.* In the case of mortal sin, it is both eternal and temporal; while in the case of venial sin, it is temporal only.

Eternal punishment consists in the condemnation of the sinner to the endless pains of Hell; that is, everyone who dies with an unforgiven mortal sin on his soul is condemned to suffer forever in "the Hell of fire, in the unquenchable fire, where the worm (of conscience) shall never die, and where it shall be salted with fire" (Mark 9:42). This punishment, however, is not the same for all mortal sins, but varies greatly in degree and intensity according to the special malice that inheres in each separate sin.

Temporal punishment consists in that punishment which must be endured for a greater or smaller period of time only, either in this life or in Purgatory. In this life, it is made up of the various temporal evils by which we are commonly afflicted, such as sickness, poverty and persecution and of voluntary works of penance; while in the next it is made up of the pains which are inflicted in Purgatory.

Whenever a mortal sin is pardoned through a good confession or an act of perfect contrition, both the guilt and the eternal punishment of the sin are entirely remitted; also, when a venial sin is pardoned, the guilt is taken away. But the temporal punishment, both of mortal and of venial sin, is remitted in each case only in proportion to the dispositions of the repentant sinner. If his sorrow is perfect and very intense, he may succeed in canceling the whole debt at once, as no doubt was the case when St. Mary Magdalen knelt at the feet of Jesus and gave free vent to her tears of perfect repentance; but if his sorrow is only imperfect, he will obtain only as much remission of punishment as corresponds to the degree of his sorrow. Now, whatever portion of temporal punishment is not remitted at the time the sin is pardoned must be canceled afterwards, either in this life by means of penitential works, or hereafter by enduring the pains of Purgatory.

Application of These Truths

With these truths before you, make a study of your past sinfulness. Have you ever taken pains to consider that the total amount of the temporal punishment that is charged against you is likely to be far greater than you suspect? And this for two reasons: First, because every sin you commit drags after it its own proportionate punishment; and second, because you may have rendered yourself guilty of a great number of sins. As to the first, you must know that punishment follows sin as necessarily as a shadow follows an object in the sunlight. A speck of dust, a tiny hair, a pencil, a tree, a house, a mountain, each casts a shadow of a particular size. So also every sin, from the smallest imperfection up to the most heinous crime a man can commit, incurs a penalty that corresponds exactly to the degree of its malice.

Just how great the punishment is in each case, we have no means of knowing; that is God's secret. But this much we do know, that in the case of mortal sins it is very great, as also in the case of those venial sins which are so close to the border-line between mortal and venial sins that the most learned theologian cannot decide whether they are still venial or have overstepped the line and are mortal.

As to the second, your total debt of temporal punishment may be exceedingly large on account of the great number of mortal and venial sins you may have committed. To convince yourself of this, sit down and examine yourself impartially as to your past life. Do not recoil from making a searching inquiry into the true state of your soul. It will not be a pleasant task, but it will be a very useful one. Perhaps it is a very necessary one. It will help you to see yourself as you really are in the sight of the all holy God, whom you cannot deceive, even though you may long have been deceiving yourself as to the true state of your soul. Such an inquiry will enable you to forestall the terrors of your judgment after death by making it possible for you to correct now what you will no longer be able to correct then.

Try then to recall all the mortal sins you have committed since you first came to the use of reason. In how many ways have you sinned grievously in thought, desire, word, action and omission of duty? Have you never missed Mass on days of obligation, eaten meat on forbidden days, or worked unnecessarily on the Lord's Day? Have you never injured your neighbor in his person, property, or good name? Have you never been guilty of serious hatred, enmity, revenge, or calumny and detraction? Have you never committed sins of impurity in thought, imagination, desire, look, speech, reading or action, alone or with others. If you have ever been guilty of any of these sins, or of others not mentioned here, though it were but once, then you must know that at this very moment a debt of temporal punishment may be charged against you.

Next try to count up all the venial sins you have so far committed. You will find them so numerous that they exceed the numbers of hairs on your head. There are the countless prayers that you have neglected to say, and those that you said with wilful distractions; there are your innumerable acts of unkindness, envy, jealousy, hatred and petty revenge; your sins of sinful gossip, tale bearing and detraction; improper words and conversation; disobedience, vanity, pride and contempt of others; and all the countless little sins inseparable from the soft, selfish, worldly and unmortified life you have been leading. In addition, there are those failures of which you are not conscious, but for which you will nevertheless have to give an account because they spring from your unwillingness to render to God that perfect service which He demands of you. How astonished and terrified you would be if you could see your soul as it is in the sight of God!

It may not be out of place in this connection to draw attention to sins of thought, desire and imagination. People frequently are of the opinion that they do not commit sin unless they *do* some forbidden action or *omit* some duty that is commanded. The truth is that every sin a man commits is first committed in thought or desire. He who deliberately dwells on sinful things, entertains, for example, unchaste thoughts or desires, or thoughts of hatred and revenge, is guilty of sin the very instant the will gives its approval to the forbidden thing. The external action is not necessary. "Everyone that shall look upon a woman to lust after her, hath already committed adultery with her in his heart" (Matt. 5:28). Many more sins are committed by thought and desire than by action and omission. Hence in the sight of men a man may appear very respectable, while in the sight of God he may be a veritable sink of iniquity.

Your conscience resembles an unused darkened room. As long as the light is excluded, you cannot tell whether it is clean or dusty. But the moment you open the blinds and let the bright sunlight in, you are surprised to find that the floor and the furniture are overlaid with a thick coat of dust and that even the air is filled with myriads of dust particles. This is a true picture of your soul. Never having examined yourself thoroughly, you imagine that you are well-nigh sinless, and perhaps you are secretly congratulating yourself that you "are not as the rest of men," full of sins and faults; but if you scrutinize your conscience in the bright light of God's grace, you will be alarmed at the sight that will greet your eyes. Your sins will seem to outnumber the millions of particles of dust that have accumulated in a room which has not been dusted for weeks.

True, you hope that all your mortal and many of your venial sins have been forgiven. We will grant that they are forgiven. But then you must remember that the pardon of a sin does not necessarily always include the canceling of its temporal punishment. This depends, as we have seen, on the perfection of your sorrow and the amount of penance you have done. Now did you ever have *perfect* sorrow? And how much penance have you done? Have you done enough penance to atone for *all* your sins? Or have you not rather been satisfied with the hurried and hasty performance of the few prayers imposed on you in the sacrament of Penance? Hence, many an old unpaid debt may still be standing charged to your account.

In view of these truths, can you still pretend to be surprised if God allows various sufferings to come to you for the purpose of letting you feel that by your sins you have rendered yourself guilty of great ingratitude and irreverence toward Him? Can you reasonably expect that you should enjoy the privilege, as it were, of offending Him freely by your sins? Is He to stand by patiently, put up with your insults, and let you go unpunished? Can it be that you look for an exemption which was not granted to saints? Was not Moses punished for his sin of doubt by not being permitted to enter the Promised Land? Did not David suffer the loss of his favorite son in punishment of his sin of adultery and murder? And was not Zacharias, the father of St. John the Baptist, struck dumb for nearly a year because he doubted the word of the angel who announced to him the Precursor's birth?

No, justice demands that you be made to feel at least some portion of the temporary punishment merited by your sins, especially if you neglect to offer to God the satisfaction of voluntary works of penance.

Six

Sixth Reason:
A Substitute for Purgatory

The sixth reason why you are visited with suffering of various kinds is this: God desires to preserve you from the extremely painful and entirely unmeritorious sufferings of Purgatory.

Enough has been said in the foregoing section to show that you may be under obligation of discharging a heavy debt of temporal punishment. Just how much atonement you must make, we have no means of knowing; but considering the vast number of your sins and the various degrees of their guilt, you have every reason to believe that this debt is considerable. But now you must know that your penalty must be canceled to the last penny before you can be admitted to the unveiled presence of the God of infinite holiness.

To make the necessary payment of this debt, two ways are open to you. If you desire, you may make it in this life; if you neglect to make it in this life, you must make it in the next. There is no other alternative.

But perhaps you have often thought, and even declared, that you are quite willing to wait until after death and then in Purgatory make all the satisfaction required of you, but that you want to be excused from making it in this life. If, unconsciously, you have entertained such sentiments, you have displayed a woeful lack of knowledge as to the true nature of Purgatory.

In the first place, you do not seem to know that the smallest measure of suffering in Purgatory is far more intense than the severest pains on earth. The saints tell us that the intensity of the pain caused by the fire of Purgatory is the same as that which is caused by the fire of Hell. The only difference is this: That the souls in Purgatory are consoled by the knowledge that their torment will end sooner or later, whereas the damned in Hell are tortured by despair at the knowledge that their punishment will last forever.

In the second place, you seem to be ignorant of the fact that the advantages of present sufferings over future ones are great beyond measure. Are you aware that in this life you can accomplish vastly more in a few hours than you could in Purgatory perhaps in ever so many years? You need only attend to the following points:

1. Cultivate an ardent love of God and an abiding sorrow for all the sins of your life. For this purpose accustom yourself to make frequent acts of the love of God and of contrition.
2. Accept all your afflictions with sentiments of profound humility, in the spirit of penance, and with the conviction that only for the great mercy of God you might even now be condemned to the endless pains of Hell.
3. Unite yourself continually with Our Lord dying on the cross for love of you, and beg Him to accept your sufferings in union with His as an atonement for all your sins. The more fervently you cultivate these dispositions, the more quickly will you cancel your debt of temporal punishment. In this way you may do more in one short hour now than might be possible in Purgatory in an entire century. It all depends on the fervor of your love and the depth of your sorrow for sin.

In the third place, you must above all know that the sufferings of Purgatory are entirely unmeritorious. This means, that no matter how intensely the soul suffers there, nor how long, though it were for a thousand years, she cannot thereby procure for herself so much as a single new degree of merit by which to increase her glory in Heaven. With all her pain such a soul cannot earn for herself as much as you can by patiently bearing an insult, or suffering the prick of a pin, or denying yourself the pleasures of a dance or a movie or an ice cream soda. All that a soul in Purgatory is able to do is to cancel by slow degrees the whole debt of her punishment, that part excepted which God in His mercy remits by reason of the prayers and good works offered for her by the faithful on earth. But as to merit, the opportunity for gaining that is gone forever; it ended at the moment the soul quitted the body.

These considerations will convince you of the wonderful advantages of present over future sufferings. Whatever you endure in this life, besides its power to atone for your sins, has great efficacy for making you rich in grace and glory. Moment by moment, day by day, and year by year, you are at one and the same time canceling your debt and amassing additional claims to greater happiness in Heaven; and the more numerous and painful your sufferings, the more abundant and varied will be your merits. Considered in this light, tell me, is it not a great privilege and a precious grace to have your Purgatory here on earth? Picture to yourself how greatly a soul in Purgatory would rejoice if God permitted her to return to earth and take up your life with its pains and labors and griefs and sorrows. How she would welcome every form of suffering and embrace it gladly and try to make the most of it for atonement and for merit. But the opportunity will never be granted.

See then how unreasonable it is to complain and murmur against Divine Providence when trials and afflictions are sent to you. Revive your faith, and you will soon learn how to bless and thank God amid even the greatest agonies of pain; you will clearly understand that it is His infinite love for you and your eternal glory that makes Him lay these crosses on your shoulders.

Seven

Seventh Reason:
The Body's Share in Making Atonement

The seventh reason why you must suffer, especially in body, is this: As your body and its members and organs have been the instruments of your sins, it is but just that they be made the instruments of the expiation and atonement required for these sins. In addition to what has been said about the necessity of full atonement for your sins, we must now say a few words about the just distribution of the sufferings by which atonement must be made.

All the actions which you perform, both good and bad, you perform as a man, that is, as a human person composed of soul and body. Both your soul and your body take an intimate and necessary part in everything you do. At no time in your life do you perform a human act, that is, one for which you are responsible to God, in your body alone or in your soul alone. In every sin, therefore, that you commit, some bodily member participates. You cannot think an evil thought, entertain a sinful desire or fancy, speak a sinful word, do a forbidden act or omit a duty without the cooperation of some part of your body, which received the largest amount of pleasure and enjoyment from certain sins.

Let us consider this point in detail. There are your countless sins of thought, imagination and desire — your brain took an active part in them all. There are your equally countless sins of speech – unkind and uncharitable, bitter and malicious words and conversations; your profanations of God's Holy

Name; your suggestive and immodest jokes and stories; your lies, calumnies and detractions – your tongue was the chief instrument of them. There may be sins of gluttony, intemperance, the love of good cheer, "making a god of your belly" (Philip3:19) – the pleasures of these sins were not confined to your palate only, but extended to your whole body. You may have been guilty of immodesty in dress, by which you made yourself a walking temptation and an occasion of sin to all who chanced to see you. It was your body, consecrated in Baptism to the exclusive service of God, that you gave over to the Devil to use as an instrument for the ruin of immortal souls. And finally, if you indulged in sins of impurity and immodesty, alone or with others, it was your body and its members that reveled in forbidden pleasures. In short, there is not one of your members or senses that has not at sometime or other been enlisted in the service of sin.

Now, with these facts before you, judge for yourself whether it would be just if your soul were required to make full satisfaction in Purgatory for the sins you commit here on earth, while your body, so often the chief culprit, enjoyed complete exemption from this task. Would it be right if your soul, which frequently yields only with reluctance to the cravings of your body for sensual enjoyment, were made to pay the whole penalty, while the body, which riotously reveled in such enjoyment, escaped altogether the chastisement it so richly deserved? Surely not. For while the soul would be making a slow and painful expiation in the flames of Purgatory, the body would merely be undergoing the corruption of the grave of which it is quite unconscious. In this way it would be enjoying the privilege of complete exemption from the punishment of those many sins of which it was the necessary instrument. Again, would this be just and fair?

If, therefore, you are suffering in your body, if you are afflicted in your eyes which so often looked on sinful objects, in your ears which so greedily listened to uncharitable or immodest talk, in your head which so often was filled with wilful unholy thoughts, in your hands which you employed in so many sinful actions, in your feet which carried you to the occasions of sin or to the haunts of vice and shame, or if you suffer in any other member of your body, then humble yourself, acknowledge and adore the infinite justice of God, which now makes you expiate your sins in those very members which you used so shamefully in "making them members of iniquity," and then resolve to endure your sufferings in the spirit of penance.

At the same time you must try to realize that it is the will of God that you derive much good from what appears to be so great an evil. Remember that the sufferings you must now endure may serve you to secure a double gain; First, you can make full payment of your temporal punishment, and thus escape the torments of Purgatory; and second, God has been pleased to ordain that if you now make these same members the instruments of penance the rest of your life, they will in Heaven be transformed in glory, each one according to the amount of penitential works performed by it.

Eight

Eighth Reason:
Your Need of Conversion

The eighth reason why you are suffering may be this: God, Who desires your eternal salvation above all things, is doing all in His power to snatch you from the grave peril in which you are of losing your soul. He is trying to bring about your conversion from a life of sin to a life of grace and virtue.

God wants you in Heaven. He desires most ardently that you should succeed in winning that brilliant crown of most wondrous glory which He has so generously prepared for you from all eternity. Now, it may be that the state of your soul is such that, were you to die as you are, you could not possibly be admitted into Heaven, but your lot would be to dwell forever in "the exterior darkness, where there is weeping and gnashing of teeth." In other words, you may be living in the state of mortal sin.

Possibly you are living in open enmity with God. You may be one of those whom Sacred Scripture calls "fools"; one of those who make the silly boast that they do not believe that such a being as God exists. You may be a pretended atheist or unbeliever. I say *pretended*, because no man who uses his reason aright can honestly believe that there is no God. All such who deny God, merely wish He did not exist. With them the wish is father to the thought. The desire to be free from the restraints of the Ten Commandments so as to be able to gratify their passions without having the fear of Hell constantly hanging over their heads, is what prompts so-called atheists and unbelievers to be so loudmouthed in trying to convince the world that

God does not exist. If you who read these lines should happen to be one of these "fools who say in their hearts (not in their intellects), there is no God," then you are living in open enmity with Him, and therefore in peril of eternal damnation.

Or, you may belong to another class of sinners. Perhaps you are an "ought-to-be," that is, a fallen-away Catholic, one who has given up the practice of his religion. You happened to find in your Faith an obstacle to success and advancement in the world, in business, society or politics. Or you may have had trouble with the strict moral law of the Gospel and found the keeping of the Commandments too difficult. People usually have greater difficulties with the Commandments, especially the sixth and the ninth, than with all the truths and mysteries proposed to their belief. Or you may have become entangled in an unlawful marriage, or have drifted into bad company, or joined secret and condemned societies. Be the case as it may, your life may thus have been one of infidelity to God, and therefore full of sins of all kinds, so that you are living in the danger of eternal damnation.

Or possibly, you belong to a third class of sinners. Outwardly you have not given up your Faith, but you have committed so many sins that they outnumber the hairs of your head. There may be your neglected Masses and sacraments; your curses and oaths and blasphemies; your sins of anger, hatred and revenge; your gluttony and intemperance; your sins of impurity in thought, desire, word and action; your sins of scandal by which you inflicted spiritual murder on souls for whom Christ died a most painful death on the Cross; your lies, detractions and calumnies; your dishonesty and injustice – in one word, your complete disregard of the law of God. The greater part of your life is being wasted in mortal sin, and the danger of being condemned forever follows you like your shadow. Or finally, your life may be one of secret sinfulness. In the eyes of men, who can judge only your exterior, you pass as a model Christian, but in the eyes of God, Who searches the inmost recesses of the heart, you are a whited sepulcher, full of hidden iniquity. One or another of the following examples may fit your case:

There are not a few persons, young and old, married and unmarried, who, as every experienced missionary and retreat master knows only too well, and as every mission and retreat brings to light, are living in the unhappy state of mortal sin (though outwardly they seem to be very pious and virtuous), because they are receiving the sacraments unworthily. They go to confession regularly and frequently, but it is a mere routine performance. They are not converted. They have not the intention to break with sin. There are young people who are addicted to grievous sins, especially impurity, and continue to frequent the occasion of these sins, such as bad books, dances, parties, theaters and in particular, sinful company. They go to confession and to Holy Communion with great regularity; but unfortunately each reception of a sacrament involves them in greater guilt before God. True conversion includes the firm resolve to put away the wilful occasion of mortal sin. Without this there is no forgiveness.

Then, there are married persons, not a few, who, notwithstanding their monthly or weekly confession, continue with cold deliberation to sin grievously against the holy state of matrimony, or against the sacredness of the right to life which God has given to their offspring. Acting upon neo-pagan standards of morality, they presume to thwart God's will as to what lives they shall bring into the world, and to accomplish their evil designs, they do not shrink from committing the most heinous crimes. In the eyes of their fellowmen they may enjoy a measure of respect; they may be considered God-fearing and virtuous people; they may be active church workers or even be known as pillars of their church; but in the eyes of Him Who reads the hearts of men, they are guilty of secret abominations which cry to Heaven for vengeance, and of a sacrilegious abuse of the sacraments.

And lastly, there are those who live in mortal sin for months and often years, and all that time receive the sacraments unworthily, simply because they were ashamed or afraid to confess a grievous sin.

Supposing, now, that you should happen to be in one or another of the classes of sinners here described, then you must once and for all understand that nothing under Heaven can save you from eternal Hellfire except a thorough and perfect conversion. There is for you no other means of salvation. You must repent and obtain from God the pardon of your sins.

But now the great question arises: How will this necessary conversion be brought about? If in the past the ordinary calls of God's grace have failed to bring you to your senses, is there any hope that they will do so in the future and make you seek reconciliation with God? Nothing is more improbable. Every new sin you commit widens the chasm which separates you from God, and every new sacrilege hardens your heart more and more, until it becomes so callous that even the most astounding miracle might leave you unmoved. To convince yourself, study the case of Judas. He was lost, though he was a companion of Our Lord and an apostle. In spite of his nearness to the Author of salvation, his infidelity to grace led him to betray his Master, and to end his life by suicide. "It were better for that man if he had not been born." The miserable lot of this unhappy disciple might easily be yours too. Without an exceptional grace of God, even on your deathbed you might remain unconverted – for the reception of the last sacraments would be no guarantee whatever that you had really repented – and thus your doom would be irrevocably sealed.

But happily for you, God loves you too dearly despite your waywardness, to abandon you to such a miserable lot. He leaves nothing undone to save you even against your perverse will. But He well knows that the state of your soul is so desperate that heroic treatment and desperate remedies must be used if you are to be saved from eternal death. Hence, these present afflictions which are causing you so much suffering. Those sharp, smarting pains, and that grief and anguish which you are enduring, are designed to make you reflect seriously on the infinitely greater sufferings which are inflicted on the soul and body of the lost sinner in Hell – sufferings which are endless in duration. Those prolonged agonies, which give you no rest day and night, are indispensable to rouse you from your sinful state and make you plead for mercy, grace and salvation before it is too late. God does not willingly see you suffer, and it is only with reluctance that He afflicts you. His great love for you constrains Him to act in this manner. And since love is the motive, He will not send you more pain than needed for the cure of your soul and its restoration to health. He uses just the right measure, neither more nor less, even as a skillful surgeon cuts away only as much diseased tissue as he finds necessary for the saving of his patient's life.

This explains that heavy financial loss or that complete ruin of a prosperous business which has reduced you to a state of poverty and want; that sad bereavement which has snatched from you one of several dearly beloved children, or your cherished husband or wife; that disastrous accident or lingering illness which keeps you stretched on a bed of unabating pain for weeks and perhaps months; that loss of good name which you suffered through unkind gossip, calumny or detraction; that estrangement from friends caused by some misunderstanding or the malicious plotting of enemies, that round of sickness in your family which is piling up doctor's and druggist's bills. These are proofs, not of God's anger, but of His fatherly love for you and of His ardent desire to rescue you by all means from your self chosen danger of eternal perdition. He wants to save you and have you eternally happy with Him in Heaven.

Be wise, then, and accept those crosses with the proper disposition, so that they may fully accomplish the work for which they are sent. They will lead you to true conversion. They will help you to conceive sincere sorrow for your sins and to seek their forgiveness in the sacrament of Penance. In this way will those extremely bitter and nauseating remedies which the heavenly Physician is administering to you save you from the endless torments of Hell.

Nine

Ninth Reason:
Your Need of Perfect Conversion

The ninth reason why you are visited with various afflictions may be this: It is possible that you stand in need of perfect conversion not from the state of mortal sin perhaps, but from a life of worldliness and tepidity.

After reading what is contained in the last section you may perhaps be inclined to say: "Thank God I do not belong to any of those classes of sinners."

Yet, it may be that you stand sorely in need of thorough conversion. And why? Because you may be living in that most dangerous state of tepidity or lukewarmness which in a certain sense is more to be feared than the state of mortal sin.

What is the exact nature of the service you are rendering God? Do you take pains to avoid not only all mortal sins, but also all deliberate venial sins? Or are you heedless about the latter simply because you consider them trifles? Are you taking measures to guard against infection by the spirit of the world as you guard against infection by virulent disease, or is your soul literally mildewed and worm-eaten by the worldliness that dominates our neo-pagan society? Are you perhaps one of those who are trying to make the foolish experiment of reconciling what Our Lord declared could not be reconciled, namely, the service of two masters at one and the same time? Are you in any way enslaved to the three great lusts mentioned by St. John – the lust of the eyes, the lust of the flesh and the pride of life (I John 2:16) – even while you flatter yourself that your service to God is so perfect that there is no room for further improvement?

Thus it is quite possible that you are a slave to the lust of the eyes, the inordinate love of the goods of this world. True, you may not be aiming to make millions, but you may be trying to make a great deal more than you require for the decent maintenance of yourself and your family. The itch to get all the money you can, may have taken hold of your soul. To succeed in your plans, you do not hesitate to use unjust or at least doubtful means, and then try to justify yourself by saying that all others are doing the same thing, and what everybody does, cannot be so very wrong. Do you really believe that it is possible for men to change God's invariable standards of right and wrong merely by universally adopting the false standards prompted by avarice and greed?

Again, are you thoroughly honest in your work or business, or in the civil, political, or other office you may be holding? Do you pay a just wage to your employees, or, if you are a worker, do you do an honest day's work for a just wage? Do you perform works of mercy and piety, and give liberal alms according to your means? Closely scrutinize your conduct in these respects and see if the love of money and temporal goods is not slowly benumbing your soul and making it wholly insensible to heavenly things, yea, even making you ready to sell it and send it over to the torments of Hell.

Or, it may be that you are enslaved to the lust of the flesh. Not that you indulge in gross sins of impurity, but you lead a life of unmortified softness, a life of unrestrained enjoyment of every pleasure that the Devil and the world offer you and money enables you to procure. Possibly you never deny yourself anything, but enjoy everything that comes your way. Thus your whole life stands in direct opposition to the solemn declaration of Our Lord: "If any man will come after me, let him deny himself, take up his cross daily and follow me" (Luke 23) – and the way He walked is the way of Calvary "For whosoever will save his life, shall lose it; and he that shall lose his life for

My sake shall find it" (Luke 9:24). Ponder well the meaning of these words. If you avoid self denial, practice no self restraint, pamper your body, live in ease and luxury, and freely enjoy the pleasures of this life you will thereby endanger your eternal salvation but if you deny yourself, suffer for the sake of virtue, even to the extent of laying down your life rather than consent to sin, you will obtain life, that is, the endless glory of Heaven.

In this connection the words of a prominent churchman deserve to be quoted at length:

> "We are in danger lest our superabundant wealth should create a material civilization, so advanced, so refined, and carried out with such extraordinary subtlety of invention that it will need a very strong and firm will not to be softened by it. There is no doubt that in dress, in pleasure and in amusements there is an invasion of luxury in our higher society, which is very dangerous, and for this reason: When people have allowed themselves to go up to the brink of all that is lawful, it is very easy to trespass and go over the line that is forbidden. The line between what is lawful and unlawful in such minds is very faint and shadowy, and those who are always walking upon the brink of a precipice will not be long before they go over. The Apostle, speaking of women, says: "She that lives in pleasures, is dead while she is living" (I Tim:5). The taint of mortality is upon a refined and luxurious life though on the outside, like the whited sepulcher, it seems unspotted. There is no doubt that the precept of the Apostle is very necessary in our day and in our country: "All things are lawful to me, but all things are not expedient (I Cor. 6:12). Apply this to dress, to pleasures, to amuse-

ments, to the expenditure you make on yourself, to your domestic and private life, and you
will find a wide field for its application."
(Card. Manning, *The Four Great Events of the
Day,* p. 57).

What gives special force to these words is that they were
written before the advent of the phonograph, radio broadcast-
ing, the automobile, the moving pictures, and the countless
other inventions of current times, which minister so exten-
sively to man's natural craving for sensual enjoyment, and thus
become a mighty factor in promoting among the masses that
total forgetfulness of God and of eternal things which is so
characteristic of our age.

Those who still value their souls, should once for all
understand that it is impossible to unite a life of genuine
virtue and piety with the uncurbed enjoyment of the many
pleasures which modern commerce, scientific inventions, and
the various arts place within easy reach of even the poorest.
The words of Our Lord have not lost their original meaning:
"Enter ye in at the narrow gate: for wide is the gate and broad
is the way that leadeth to destruction; and many there are who
go in thereat. How narrow is the gate and straight is the way
that leadeth to life; and few there are that find it" (Matt. 7:13).
And the words of St. Paul are still true: "If you live according
to the flesh, you shall die; but if by the Spirit you mortify the
deeds of the flesh, you shall live" (Rom. 8:13).

Lastly, your life may be full of pride, self-sufficiency and
ambition. Perhaps your great aim is to become prominent in
business, society, or politics, but finding that your religion
stands in the way, you temporize with it, hide it, or simply
brush it aside as useless or as a nuisance. You will not let it
keep you from attaining the object of your desires. For the
purpose of gaining the good will of those from whom you
hope to receive favors, you do not scruple to support sectari-
an, and sometimes anti-Catholic endeavors; you join con-

demned societies; you send your children to institutions where God and religion are excluded and where immorality is rampant; you take an active part in worse than pagan social functions, such as shameless and immoral balls, dances, banquets and the like. Perhaps you contend that there is a two-fold standard of morality, one of rigor for the poor and uneducated, who are to put a strict interpretation on the law of God, and one of laxity for the rich and the learned, who may consider themselves dispensed from whatever is unpleasant and painful to flesh and blood in the keeping of the Commandments.

Examine also your attitude toward the word of God, toward the Church, her ministers, and her laws and regulations. Is it marked by humble obedience or by proud criticism? Do you endeavor, especially before your non-Catholic friends, to smooth over and soften down the hard and painful truths of the Gospel, for example, the sinfulness of heresy or of false worship or of indifferentism which claims that one religion is as good as another, and especially the doctrine of eternal damnation. Do you carp at the Church because she excommunicates those who read works dangerous to faith and morals and those who join forbidden societies; because she reprobates mixed marriages, and condemns godless systems of education? Do you find fault with her because in your opinion she is "not liberal and progressive" enough, and refuses to yield a hair's breadth in points of morality, as for example, in regard to divorce and race suicide?

Now, if an impartial examination reveals to you that you are guilty of any of the points mentioned in this section, then you must conclude that you are infected with the disease of tepidity. The three great lusts are holding you in their coils. What else does this imply but that you are in danger of losing your soul? Your present condition is slowly but surely preparing you for a complete break with God sooner or later, for "you cannot serve two masters."

This makes it plain that you are sorely in need of thorough conversion just as if you were steeped in the grossest forms of mortal sin. You must "renounce the world, the flesh and the Devil," as you promised to do in Baptism, and begin to serve God with an undivided and eternal allegiance.

To make it possible for you to accomplish this hard work, God is mercifully lending you His aid. By means of painful sufferings He is trying to bring you to a sense of your duty. They are designed to wean you from your love of the world and its inane delights, and make you foster a deep and lasting hatred for the things that have hitherto been the cause of innumerable sins. He wants you to become practically convinced of the absolute necessity of a life of penance. "Unless you do penance, you shall all likewise perish" (Luke 13:2).

Try then to see God's infinite love manifested in the afflictions He sends you. Do you not see that, only for the sufferings you endure, you would become so bewitched by the vain and fleeting pleasures of this life that you would cast all care of your eternal salvation to the winds? Pain has opened Heaven to thousands who otherwise would have been lost without fail.

Ten

Tenth Reason:
Forestalling the Danger of Eternal Perdition

The tenth reason why you must suffer may be this: God, Whose knowledge of your future is as perfect as is His knowledge of your past and your present, foresees that a life without the cross would infallibly be the cause of your eternal damnation.

Were you to see a child which betrayed strong inclinations to lying, stealing or cruelty, and was never corrected by its overindulgent parents, but rather petted and even encouraged in its evil tendencies, you could predict with a fair degree of certainty that the child will turn out to be a criminal and end its life in the penitentiary or on the gallows. True, nothing may be further from the child's mind than such an outlook; the child may glory in its freedom from wholesome restraint; but you who know something of human nature and the history of crime can make a fairly accurate forecast of the child's career.

And so, perhaps, God foresees that a long life, robust health, brilliant talents, honors, prosperity, wealth, success in business or politics or social life, will prove to be the cause of your eternal damnation. Unknown to and unsuspected by yourself there are lurking in your character all kinds of evil tendencies, fortunately as yet in a state of abeyance. They are lying dormant within you mainly because favorable opportunities for their development have so far been wanting. Should these opportunities come your way, should you happen to be placed in other circumstances, these dormant tendencies may awaken and grow into passions so strong and so violent as to get entirely beyond your control. Before long you might find yourself driven headlong into the commission of sins and crimes such as you would never have thought yourself capable of committing.

In the light of these truths, we will proceed to show that misfortunes are often great blessings, inasmuch as they preserve many a man from the misfortunes of eternal perdition.

The Condition of the Poor

Look about you and see what evils often accompany the possession of wealth. Do we not meet with Catholics who were fervent and devout as long as they remained poor or moderately comfortable, but became lukewarm in the practice of their faith, or even gave it up altogether, just as soon as fortune began to smile upon them and riches came their way? From that time they considered themselves emancipated from the service of God. They no longer felt the need of prayer and of the sacraments, since their money enabled them to procure so much of what they craved. Now the almighty dollar is the god whom they worship and on whom they rely.

Or, if they do not openly break with the Church, and continue to discharge their most essential Christian duties, they do it in a way that makes the impression that they are doing a favor to God by condescending to appear in church and bend their knee before the altar. Their newly acquired wealth is spent, not for the glory of God, but in selfish enjoyment. They never give it even a passing thought that it is their duty to assist and relieve the needy and poor. In fact, they have only contempt for the poor. They pride themselves in the thought, and even the declaration, that they belong to "the better class of Catholics," forgetting that the poor are the privileged ones in the Church of God.

The Catholic atmosphere that once prevailed in their homes is no longer felt there. There are no more family prayers, no books of instruction, no religious ornaments, such as crucifixes, pictures of the saints, holy water. These things might offend their non-Catholic friends, and besides, they savor of superstition. At the same time there is a profusion of pagan and suggestive ornaments, statues and pictures, which are a standing temptation to their children, and there are books and periodicals which abound in attacks on the Church and reek with immorality. The children no longer go to the parochial school, for that is not fashionable enough. They must attend some godless secular school. What matters it if their faith and purity suffer shipwreck there?

In a word, often, as wealth grows, faith wanes, and by and by religion is put aside as something altogether useless for getting on in the world.

Now, this lot might very easily befall you, or your children, were you to be blessed – or should we say cursed? – with an abundance of the goods of this world. And what would be the outcome? A calamity than which none can be greater – the condemnation of your soul to the fire of Hell. God foresees all perfectly. And loving you with a most affectionate love, and desiring nothing more ardently than your eternal happiness with Him in Heaven, He has mercifully kept you in poverty or moderation, to preserve you from the grave dangers of eternal perdition which are so intimately bound up with the possession of riches.

Sickness and Infirmities

It may be that you are afflicted with a defect, or a lingering and painful ailment from which you are recovering very slowly, or from which you have been told there is no recovery. Reflect a little. Might it not be that only for this accident, this sickness, or this trial of the soul, you would not be living in the happy state of grace and friendship of God, but rather in emnity with Him, and therefore in the ever present danger of eternal Hell-fire? Perhaps, only for this state of suffering, your soul might be wholly disfigured with the leprosy of sin. Your sins might be as numerous as the sands on the seashore and as red as crimson. You might be a helpless victim to the countless snares which Satan is continually setting for the ruin of souls. You might have drifted into the haunts of sin and vice, where your virtue would have been hopelessly lost. You might have become entangled in friendships resulting in the loss of the priceless jewels of innocence and faith. Instead of being a child of God and heir of Heaven, and basking in the light and warmth of the tender love of your heavenly Father, you might be wallowing in the mire of impurity and leading a life of disgrace. The sad lot of thousands of others might very easily have been yours too. And who knows, but that a life of sin might long ago have brought on your death and plunged you into Hell, out of which there is no redemption?

From this great misfortune God mercifully preserved you by means of your affliction. Weighed in the balance of Faith, have not your sufferings been to you a great blessing in disguise?

Deaths and Bereavements

One more case which many persons make an occasion for doubting God's goodness and love, and sometimes of blasphemy against His justice, must be considered in this connection. It is the grief and sorrow occasioned by the death of some dearly loved member of the family, or of a relative or friend, or of one whose life is considered a necessity for the good of the survivors. It may be an only child, or the favorite one of several children, or the father who is the only money earner in the family, or the mother of a number of small children, whom death mercilessly snatches from the home and consigns to the cold and silent tomb.

At such times, it is not rare to find persons – even such as one would expect to be models of Christian fortitude and of perfect resignation to the Divine will – who grow rebellious, and defiantly demand of God why He dared take from them one whom they loved so dearly or who was so necessary to the family. Some even go still further and make such bereavements a pretext for giving up their faith.

Now what is the true explanation of this apparent cruelty on the part of God? Again the answer is: His infinite love for His children and His great solicitude for their eternal salvation. It is for the good of the deceased that He demands this sacrifice, though at the same time He also has the good of the survivors in view. Who knows but for this seeming untimely death the dear departed one might have been sentenced to the flames of Hell? Dying when he did he won for himself the surpassing bliss of Heaven.

The key to the proper solution of this difficulty is given us in the Book of Wisdom, where the sacred writer speaks of the death of young persons in these terms:

"The just man, if he be prevented with death (i.e., if he died young), shall be in rest. For venerable old age is not that of a long time, nor counted by the number of years; but the understanding of many is gray hairs. He pleased God and was beloved; and living among sinners he was translated. He was taken away lest wickedness should alter his understanding or deceit beguile his soul. For the bewitching vanity obscureth good things, and the wandering of concupiscence overturneth the innocent mind. Being made perfect in a short space he fulfilled a long time. For his soul pleased God; therefore He hastened to bring him out of the midst of iniquities.

"But the people see this and understand not, nor lay up such things in their hearts; that the grace of God and His mercy are with His saints, and that He hath respect to His chosen ones. But the just that is dead condemneth the wicked that are living; and youth soon ended, the long life of the unjust. For they shall see the end of the wise man and shall not understand what God hath designed for him, and why the Lord hath set him in safety."

Turning Bereavements to Good Account

Let us now ask: Are you one of those who make bereavements an occasion of rebellion against God's holy will? If so, it is a great pity indeed; and that for several reasons.

First, you must be a stranger to those interior consolations which spring from the conviction that whatever God does for His children, always proceeds from infinite love and is therefore directed to their best interests. Second, you are throwing away those most excellent opportunities of growing rich in grace and merit, which are invariably linked with the trials God is pleased to send us. Third, besides sustaining this great loss you also incur a certain amount of punishment, for you cannot entertain these rebellious thoughts against God without committing sins of one kind or another. And fourth, while you pretend by your uncontrolled grief to display a great love for your departed relatives and friends, you are in reality practicing great cruelty against them. This may sound strange; but you will agree with me after reading the following.

If the souls of your departed relatives are detained in Purgatory (and very likely they are, unless they be children who died before attaining the use of reason, and in that case you should rather rejoice with them since they are in the secure possession of their eternal glory), then there is only one favor for which they crave and plead, and that is a speedy deliverance from their torments. You have it in your power to give them the relief they so piteously implore. You can open to them the portals of Heaven and allow them to enter quickly into the possession of their eternal glory. And this happiness you can procure for them by prayers, good works, Masses and the like. But of all the means by which you can help them and send them rejoicing on their way to Heaven, one of the best consists in offering up to God fervent acts of loving resignation to His adorable will, and of humble and submissive acceptance of all the sorrows which your bereavement is inflicting on you.

If this is so, is it not clear that to deny your departed relatives a help that can so speedily and so frequently be given them, and that is so effective in freeing them from their terrible sufferings, is nothing short of cruelty? Supposing the dead could come back to make a personal appeal to their friends what do you think would they say to them? Would it not be something like this: "If you truly love us, away with your immoderate grief, with your tears and wails which bring us no relief whatever! Away with these floral decorations, and these expensive funeral customs, which are more pagan than Christian and do not afford us any relief whatsoever. Help us by your prayers and good works, and above all by perfect resignation to the adorable will of the Author of life and death. All that we crave is speedy deliverance from our frightful torments, and an early admission into Heaven. Prove your love by procuring for us this precious boon."

Bereavements therefore furnish a good test as to the true character of your love for your relatives and friends.

The Timeliness of Every Man's Death

In this connection we cannot refrain from quoting a passage from the writings of the saintly Father Faber, which is not only very instructive but also very consoling. Speaking of what he calls the timeliness of every man's death, he says:

> Let us dwell on one feature of God's providence, the way in which He vouchsafes to time things. Think of the hour of death, of its surpassing importance, of its thrilling risks, of all those inward processes of which we have already spoken. Now may we not conclude, or with reasonable hope infer, that to most if not to all men the hour of their death is seasonably timed?
>
> They die when it is best for them to die. There are some dangers in advance which they avoid by dying then. They die when they are in the best state for dying. Even the deaths of those who are lost may be mercifully timed. When men die young, it is perhaps because they would have lost themselves if they had lived to

be old. When men die late, it is perhaps to give them time to correspond to grace, to do penance for the past, and especially that they may get rid of some evil habit which would else be their perdition, and which the mere infirmity of age may help them to abandon.

When men die just as they are coming into the possession of riches, or at the outset of a smiling career of laudable ambition, it is perhaps because God sees in their natural character or in their personal circumstances some seeds of future evil; and so He takes them while that evil lies innocently undeveloped in their souls.

Who can think of what death is, and yet doubt that God's wisdom and His love are brought to bear with inexpressible sweetness both on its manner and its time? If God were pleased to tell us, we would probably be amazed at the number of convincing reasons that there are why each of us should die when and where and how we do.

The very sight of so much legislation and arrangement, on the part of God, about this one final act of our probation is doubtless pouring into the souls of the blessed at all hours delightful streams of wondering adoration and ecstatic love. (Faber, *Creator and Creature,* p. 344).

Eleven

Eleventh Reason:
Making Atonement for the Sins of Others

You must have noticed, dear reader, that the ten reasons for human suffering so far considered revolve mainly about the subject of sin and its consequences. Original sin, your personal sins, atonement for the same, the forestalling of the great danger of eternal perdition in which sin places you – these furnish a number of reasons why sufferings form part and parcel of your life.

Five more reasons remain to be explained. These however, are of a different class. They assign to suffering a more exalted office than merely enduring the results of one's sins. A careful study of them will reveal the blessedness of suffering.

The eleventh reason why you must suffer, especially if you have for a long time tried to lead a virtuous life, may be this: God may have found you worthy of the noble vocation of making your life an atonement for the countless sins committed against Him the world over by His ungrateful children.

Look about you and see how exceedingly great is the number of sins that are unceasingly rising up to Heaven, day and night, challenging God to send down His condign chastisements on the sinful race of men. So numerous are these sins that they exceed the sands on the seashore. And they are also of every conceivable degree of malice. There are the sins of the vast mass of pagans who live in ignorance of God and His holy law, and there the more grievous sins of Christians who lead godless lives despite their better knowledge and their many graces. There are the sins of malice committed by those who are filled with a hatred of God, which can only be called diabolical; and there are the infidelities of those who make a profession of an exclusive service of God, but do not hesitate to offend Him in many things, even mortally, when passion craves indulgence or self-love covets some temporal advantage or gratification.

Now if God consulted only the claims of His infinite justice, it would go hard with these unfortunate sinners. His chastisements would fall crushingly on them, even as they did at the time of the deluge, or the destruction of Sodom, or of Jerusalem. Happily, however, His equally infinite mercy intervenes in their behalf. It makes Him devise ways and means for turning away from them their well merited punishment. Two great means there are that the Divine mercy has generously provided for this purpose: the holy sacrifice of the Mass, and the voluntary expiation made to Him by devout souls. Passing over here the Mass, we will consider the second means.

We find scattered throughout the world many select souls that have followed the inspiration of grace and made themselves willing victims of expiatory suffering for the love of God. The world knows little or nothing of them, for they usually lead a hidden and secluded life, as a rule known only to their confessor or spiritual director. They are leading lives of incessant expiation through patient suffering, though personally they may never have lost their baptismal innocence, or, if they were sinners once, they have, like St. Mary Magdalen, become God's special favorites by the fervor and intensity of their sorrow, love and spirit of penance. Some are made to endure cruel persecutions; others great interior trials. Others again are stricken with painful maladies, which sometimes last for years, sometimes for a lifetime. With their Divine Savior, these heroic souls are nailed to the cross, and in union with Him they endure agonies of a veritable crucifixion which knows no respite and no relief. But they are true heroes, who measure up to the demands of their sublime calling. Far from losing patience or giving way to murmuring, they are even very joyful – a condition which is a mystery to those who know nothing of the marvelous power of Divine grace. So intense is their love of God and so pained and grieved are they at seeing Him outraged by sin, that they would gladly suffer more if such were the Divine pleasure.

The expiation such souls are called upon to make is sometimes for sin in general, sometimes for sins of a particular kind. The mission of some is to satisfy for blasphemies; of others to atone for sacrileges and profanations of the Blessed Sacrament; while others again are called upon to expiate the sins of unfaithful ministers of the altar.

We have an example of such vicarious suffering in the life of Gemma Galgani, a saintly maiden of Lucca, who died in 1903. She had received the wounds of the nails and lance, as also of the crown of thorns and of the scourging of our Savior, which for some time bled every Thursday and Friday. In 1900 Our Lord said to her: Victims of expiation are needed for the sins of the world. If you could only let the world know how incensed My heavenly Father is at the world. Even now He is preparing a severe chastisement for the whole human race." Was this not perhaps a warning of the World War?

In Religious Communities

So, too, in religious communities certain members seem to have received the spiritual vocation to suffer for the good of their order. They suffer for a twofold purpose. In the first place, they have the task of atoning for the sins and infidelities of their fellow members. In this way they become a most valuable asset to the community, even though they take no active part in the special work to which the community is committed. By their continuous offering of satisfaction, they prevail with God to withhold His chastisements which might otherwise be visited upon the order as a whole or upon one or another of its houses.

In the second place, theirs is the spiritual task of procuring for their community the particular graces it needs for the success of the work assigned to it. A religious family with its particular work, such as to educate the young, to conduct missions, to train young priests, to preach the Gospel in pagan lands, stands constantly in need of a copious supply of very special graces to do the work faithfully and with fruit. These special graces are earned by means of prayer and especially by the powerful intercession of suffering. Hence the kind provision of Divine Providence, selecting certain souls whose great work it is to keep those who are fighting the battles of the Lord supplied with the graces they need while in the field.

Twelve

Twelfth Reason:
Promoting the Welfare of the Church

The twelfth reason why you must suffer, though you try to lead a good life, may be this: God may have given you the vocation of taking an active and necessary part in the promotion of the welfare of His church. You are to help to procure for her those special graces she needs continually in order to fulfill her mission of saving immortal souls.

The task of establishing on earth the kingdom of God is carried out by Mother Church under stress of innumerable difficulties. Now just as in His infinite wisdom God saw fit that the great work of man's redemption should be accomplished through the excessive sufferings which Jesus Christ endured in His passion and death on the Cross, so also He sees fit that the work of saving souls, which is nothing but the redemption continued in the world to the end of time, shall be accomplished to a great extent through painful suffering. For this purpose God selects certain souls that are especially dear to Him, and give them the vocation of procuring for His Church, by the intercession of pain, whatever special graces she needs at different times and in different places.

The lives of the saints are full of examples of heroic souls who offered themselves to God to suffer for the good of the Church. So, too, there are many souls living in the world today who make it their life's work to suffer for this same intention. Priests and missionaries find in them most helpful allies in their efforts to save souls. While they are preaching, hearing confessions, assisting the dying, and doing other apostolic work, these generous sufferers are obtaining for them those powerful graces without which their labors would often be fruitless.

In this way, these souls hidden away from the gaze of the world, are doing a wonderful work of love and zeal. Somewhere in the wide world the effects of their intercession make themselves felt; it may be thousands of miles away, on the bleak ice fields of the North, in the tropical forests of the South, in the thick jungles of Africa, amid the dense population of China, in the hovels and slums of our modern million populated cities, in hospitals, and prisons – in short, anywhere where souls are to be snatched from eternal perdition and saved unto life everlasting. It is only on the day of Judgment that it will be known how much of their success priests and missionaries owe to such intercessory suffering.

If, therefore, you should happen to be one of those to whom God has given this sublime vocation of cooperating with His ministers in the extension of His kingdom on earth, endeavor to prove yourself worthy of your noble calling. A deep sense of gratitude for the precious gift of faith should impel you to offer yourself with wholehearted generosity to suffer anything it may please Him to send you, so that the establishment of Christ's kingdom may be hastened.

Thirteen

Thirteenth Reason:
Procuring the Conversion of Sinners

The thirteenth reason why you must suffer may be this: God may have given you the vocation of procuring the grace of conversion for sinners, especially for those who are in their last agony and in danger of dying in their sins.

Take your place in spirit at the bedside of a man who is about to pass out of this life with mortal sin on his soul. A few moments more and his lot will be settled for all eternity. If he appears before the Divine Judge with his sins unforgiven - nothing can save him from the unquenchable fire of Hell. Forever and ever he must endure the most frightful torments – torments so great that in comparison with them the agonies of those who die by fire are but the merest shadows of pain.

Now, it is at this critical time that the intercession of God's friends comes in and plays a decisive role in the great drama of the sinner's death In answer to the fervent prayers which are offered up for the conversion of sinners in their last agony, and especially in consideration of the sufferings endured for this same intention by so many holy souls, God willingly grants to dying sinners such additional graces as will triumph over their obstinacy, and make them seek timely reconciliation by means of a sincere confession, or at least by an act of perfect contrition.

The decisive moment has come. Grace scores a glorious victory. The dying sinner turns to God, repents, is pardoned – is saved – saved with an eternal salvation! Who is there that can realize all that is contained in this short statement: He is saved! He has escaped Hell with all its unspeakable misery, and has been reinstated in his right and title to the surpassing bliss of Heaven. A hymn of gladness and thanksgiving is intoned among the saints and angels, who rejoice above measure that another soul has been snatched from perdition and will one day join their happy company to praise and glorify God for all eternity.

But who can have an idea of the sentiments of love and gratitude which that soul will henceforth foster towards those by whose prayers and sufferings she was rescued from the grasp of the Demon at the last moment and sent rejoicing on her way to Heaven? And how these sentiments will be intensified when she contrasts her happiness in Heaven with the misery to which she would have been condemned, had it not been for the grace of conversion procured for her by generous sufferers on earth. The gratitude that you would feel toward one who rescued you from death by fire bears no comparison with that which such a soul feels toward those who have rescued her from the endless fire of Hell.

What has here been described occurs not at rare intervals only, but thousands of times every day in the year. Nearly one hundred thousand souls pass into eternity every twenty-four hours. How many of these are saved and how many are lost, we have no means of knowing, for God has made no revelation on this point; but so much we can take for certain, that of those who are saved very many owe their salvation to the grace of conversion procured for them in the hour of death by the prayers and sufferings of the friends of God on earth.

In view of these truths, should you not cultivate an ardent desire of contributing as much as lies in your power toward the furtherance of this great work of mercy? Should you not be willing to suffer, and suffer much, that dying sinners may escape the horrors of that Hell-fire which awaits them in eternity unless they repent before death puts an end to their life?

Fourteen

Fourteenth Reason:
Acquiring Conformity with Jesus Christ

The fourteenth reason why you are enduring crosses and afflictions may be this: Because you are predestined by God to the glory of Heaven, it is necessary that you should first be conformed to the image and likeness of Jesus Christ.

In several of his epistles to the first Christians, St. Paul speaks of the necessity of conformity with Jesus Christ as a condition for obtaining the crown of eternal glory. He tells them that everyone who is predestined for Heaven must first be transformed into the image and likeness of the son of God. The resemblance which a citizen of the heavenly kingdom must bear to his King, is as perfect as grace can make it. He must become another Christ. Our heavenly Father will receive as His child him only in whom He can trace the lineaments of His eternal Son, and of whom He can testify as He testified of Him on Mount Tabor: "This is My beloved Son, in whom I am well pleased."

But Jesus Christ was a man of sorrows. From the very first moment of His early life down to His last breath on the cross He suffered incessantly both in soul and in body. His actual passion lasted only a few hours, it is true; but its anticipation, which included the clearest foreknowledge of its minutest details, accompanied Him all through life and never left Him without suffering – no, not for a single moment. There were the hatred, enmity and ill-treatment He received from His own people, His rejection as an outcast, His condemnation to an unjust death as a malefactor, and finally that unheard of cruelty with which He was nailed to the cross, there to die as though He were the worst of criminals. Lastly, there was the keen pain that was inflicted on Him by the knowledge that countless souls would be lost in spite of all He did to save them. Truly, no man was ever called upon to suffer as much as this innocent Lamb of God.

Consider next that He endured all this not from compulsion, but from an entirely voluntary choice of His own. Urged by the most tender love for your soul, He deliberately chose what caused Him pain. He suffered to the utmost limits of human endurance. Much less suffering would have been more than sufficient for your redemption; but what would have sufficed to redeem you, did not satisfy His desire to prove to you how intently He loved you. Had it been necessary, He would gladly have suffered still more. Or, supposing you were the only person in all the world that stood in need of redemption, He would most willingly have suffered for you all that He suffered for the whole human race. How the depth and immensity of our Savior's love is revealed in His desire, nay, in His burning thirst, to suffer, that you might be able to save your soul.

In view of these truths can it be a matter of surprise that it is a fixed law of the supernatural life that all who are to be admitted to the kingdom of Heaven must first become conformed to the likeness of the King? Or that Heaven must be won by the same means by which the redemption was accomplished? Or that you must be prepared to imitate the life of lowliness and suffering of your Divine Savior here on earth if you desire to be transformed by the splendor of His glory in Heaven? Hear Him say: "Ought not Christ to have suffered and so enter into His glory?"

It is significant that Our Blessed Savior took special pains to impress this hard and unwelcome doctrine on His disciples, and through them on all who aspire to the glory of Heaven. Listen to His own words: "If any one will come after me, let him deny himself, take up his cross daily, and follow me. For whosoever shall save his life shall lose it; and he that will lose his life for my sake shall save it. He that taketh not up his cross and followeth Me, is not worthy of Me."

Hear St. Paul teach the same doctrine: "You have received the Spirit of adoption of sons, whereby we cry: Abba (Father)! For the Spirit himself giveth testimony to our spirit that we are the sons of God. And if sons, heirs also; heirs indeed of God and joint heirs with Christ; yet so if we suffer with Him that we may also be glorified with Him" (Rom. 8: 15-17).

Consequently, if you are weighed down by crosses, though you have long tried to lead a life of piety and virtue and therefore imagine that you ought to be entirely free from such trials, remember that the heavenly Artist is at work transforming you by slow degrees into a perfect image of Jesus Christ.

This is true, no matter what the nature of your sufferings may happen to be; whether they come from sickness, accidents, loss of fortune or good name, or from persecution raised against you simply because you have resolved to lead a life of perfect imitation of your Divine Savior. In this last case you must reconcile yourself to the fact that it is an unchanging law that "all who will (i.e., are determined to) live godly in Christ Jesus, shall suffer persecution."

This law applies in several ways; but it applies especially to Catholics, who often must pay dearly for the precious gift of Faith by "suffering persecution for justice sake," and must be willing to bear the world's hatred and enmity for the privilege of being children of God and heirs of Heaven. Our Lord makes this truth so plain that there is no room for ignorance in regard to it. "If the world hate you," He says," know that it hath hated Me before you."

In a great variety of ways, therefore, God accomplishes the work of transforming sinful men and women into faithful likenesses of His Divine Son. If you keep these truths always in mind, they will strengthen and greatly encourage you when tempted to impatience or despondency. Never forget that you shall reign with Christ in Heaven only if you suffer with Him here on earth.

Fifteen

Fifteenth Reason:
Predestination to an Exalted Degree
of Glory in Heaven

The fifteenth and last reason why you must suffer may be this: God, who loves you with a love that surpasses all understanding, may have predestined you to enjoy for all eternity an exceptionally high degree of glory in Heaven.

If you are weighed down by heavy crosses and painful afflictions despite the fact that you have long tried to lead a sinless life and to love God above all things, it is very likely because the Divine Goodness has most wonderful designs on you for eternity.

As sun, moon and stars differ greatly in size and brilliancy, so also do the saints in Heaven differ greatly in the splendor of their glory. Our Divine Savior assures us that on the day of Judgment every man shall receive his proper recompense of good or of evil, and that in His Father's house, that is, in Heaven, there are many mansions. The glory and happiness that will be allotted to the elect will be of many varieties, both as to kind and as to degree. No doubt, there are many saints who possess what are the lowest degrees, such as infants who died after baptism before they attained the use of reason, and pagans, and life-long sinners who were converted just before death; but there are also very many who are crowned with a glory and an honor so immense that they will rank with the most exalted of the angelic choirs. Some may even be still higher. This we know is the case with the Blessed Virgin Mary, whose glory far exceeds that of all the angels and saints.

Now, may it not be that you who are reading these lines, may also be one of those whom the goodness of God has predestined to one of the highest places in Heaven? Should this be the case – and there is no reason why it may not be – then know that you can take possession of your appointed place only if at the moment of your death you have attained that degree of sanctity which is commensurate with the particular degree of glory intended for you.

This gives rise to the very important question: By what means will you manage to attain that exalted degree of holiness which will entitle you to receive this glory? A life of ordinary goodness, made up of the avoidance of sin, the saying of your daily prayers, the reception of the sacraments and the performance of good works will be insufficient. As scaling a high and steep mountain is vastly more difficult than walking to the top of a gently sloping hill, and demands strenuous and persevering efforts, so it is with the attainment of the sanctity required of those who are destined for the higher places in Heaven. Only the most heroic efforts persevered in until death will enable souls to reach the summit of the mountain of Christian perfection.

Now, it may well be that for this strenuous work you have neither the strength nor even the desire. Hence, if you were left to your initiative, you would in no way come near reaching the degree of sanctity God wants you to attain. This would mean total failure in your endeavor to win the throne and crown of glory prepared for you in Heaven.

But fortunately God is not willing to see you forego what He has so generously set aside for you, even though you are so lamentably blind to your best interests that you do not care whether you win it or not. And so He takes the sanctification of your soul in His own hands. By gentle pressure, yet without compulsion of your will, He makes you do what you have neither the courage nor the desire to undertake of your own accord. You can surmise what means He employs. It is the cross – pain, affliction, tribulation, temptation, in a word, sufferings of all kinds, which follow one upon the other in seemingly endless succession.

Here is the unraveling of a secret that has long been a puzzle to you. It explains that slow and troublesome illness which has cast you on a bed of suffering these many months or years, and perhaps bids fair to keep you there till the end of your life; it explains those cruel disappointments, that extreme poverty, those crushing humiliations, that heartless persecution, which come to you not only from your enemies, but also perhaps from your relatives, friends and superiors. It explains further those painful interior trials which are often harder to bear than bodily suffering – those persistent and violent temptations against faith or hope or charity or any other virtue; that dryness, that disgust at times for prayer, the sacraments and spiritual things in general; and finally, the hardest of all, that desolation of spirit by which it often seems to you that God has rejected and already condemned you as a reprobate to the torments of Hell. If you examine your painful state in the light of Faith, you will discover in all this apparent cruelty at the hands of God the most convincing proofs of God's tender love for you. He is preparing you to become a worthy occupant of the throne of marvelous glory He has so generously prepared for you in His kingdom.

You know that the vine must be pruned year after year if it is to bear an abundance of luscious fruit; that the diamond must undergo a slow and laborious process of grinding and polishing if it is to delight the eye with its highest degree of brilliancy; and that gold must be subjected to the action of intense heat if it is to be freed from all dross and rendered perfectly pure. So also must your soul now undergo the process, as it were, of pruning, polishing and refining, so that she may be worthy of taking her place among the most exalted choirs of angels and saints.

To make this important point still clearer, let us have recourse to numbers. Let it be supposed that to obtain the degree of glory intended for you, you stand in need of one million degrees of merit. If it depended entirely on your own efforts, you might not succeed in gaining more than half that number, and the attainment of your crown would be hopelessly beyond your reach. Something is badly needed to supply this deficiency. And what can this be? One thing only – suffering. You must acquire the balance of the necessary merits by cheerfully carrying the cross which God places on your shoulders for this purpose.

Again, the glory intended for you may correspond to several millions of degrees of merits. In that case you would not be able to amass the required amount even if you practiced the most heroic self-denial, humility, charity and the other Christian virtues. A second time God comes to your assistance. He subjects you to the ordeal of suffering to such an extent as He knows is necessary to enable you to procure the purchase price of your exalted rank in Heaven. This truth is clearly illustrated in the lives of the saints, who invariably suffered the more here on earth the higher they were to be elevated in glory hereafter. Viewed in this light do you not discover a new and deep meaning in these words of Sacred Scripture: "Whom the Lord loveth, He chastiseth; and as a father in the son He pleaseth himself"?

What wonderful joy and happiness you will experience for all eternity if you succeed in mastering the truth about suffering here explained, in all your afflictions lovingly resigning yourself to the ever blessed will of Him Who has decreed such a marvelous glory for you in the life to come. Instead of looking upon sufferings as a curse and a punishment, and murmuring against Divine Providence, try rather to welcome your trials, rejoice in them, and fervently thank God for giving you so unmistakable a pledge of His most tender love for you. If you master the truth about the real nature and uses of sufferings, you will soon think of them as the saints did, and instead of praying to be delivered from them, you will, after their example, even pray for more. "Lord, not to die, but to suffer," was the heroic prayer of St. Teresa.

The Day of Eternity

Before concluding, let us ask you to transport yourself in spirit to Heaven, that kingdom of matchless glory where God shall reign forever, surrounded by unnumbered legions of bright angelic spirits and millions upon millions of happy saints. These last, who on earth had the good sense to live by faith, who despised things temporal for the sake of gaining life eternal, who waged a life-long war against their evil inclinations and unruly passions in order to render to God a perfect service of love, and who cheerfully embraced the sufferings to which they were subjected – these shall now for all eternity rejoice in the undisturbed possession of glory, peace and happiness that no human mind can fathom or comprehend. Oh, how blessed they are now in enjoying so securely what they hoped and labored for on earth with such implicit trust and confidence in God's unfailing promises! Forever and ever they shall experience the truth of the words of St. Paul: "Eye hath not seen, ear hath not heard, nor hath it entered into the heart of man what things God hath prepared for those that love Him." Truly, "the sufferings of their earthly life were not worthy to be compared with the glory that is now revealed in them."

Sixteen

The Saints: Our Models

The Holy Man Job

A name that has become a synonym not only for human suffering in its worst form, but also for perfect patience and resignation to the adorable will of God amid the greatest afflictions, is that of the holy man Job.

Sacred Scripture describes this great servant of God as a man who "was simple and upright, fearing God and avoiding evil." He had seven sons and three daughters, and was blessed with a great abundance of riches. But in the midst of his prosperity it pleased God to put his virtue to a severe test. By a series of calamities Job lost all his children and all his temporal possessions. But he stood this test admirably. Not a word of complaint or of murmuring against Divine Providence escaped his lips. His only comment was: "Naked I came out of my mother's womb and naked shall I return thither; the Lord gave, and the Lord hath taken away. As it hath pleased the Lord, so is it done; blessed be the name of the Lord." And the sacred writer adds: "In all these things Job sinned not with his lips, nor spoke he anything foolish against God."

But these afflictions, great as they were, were by no means the full measure of his sufferings. God allowed Satan to "strike him with a very grievous ulcer from the sole of the foot to the top of the head; and he took a potsherd and scraped the corrupt matter, sitting on a dunghill." But even so great a misery as this could not provoke him to murmur against God. On the very contrary, when his wife, less virtuous than he, ridiculed him for his immovable trust in God, he reproved her with these words: "Thou hast spoken like one of the foolish women. If we have received good things at the hands of God, why should we not receive evil?" In all these things Job sinned not with his lips.

In this way did holy Job become a model of unfaltering trust in God and of perfect patience and resignation to the decrees of Divine Providence for all future generations. What is still more remarkable about him is that he practiced this wonderful resignation though he had not before him, as we have, the example of Jesus Christ, the model Sufferer, and that he bore his afflictions in so heroic a manner though he had not at his disposal the special graces that we have in the Church, especially through the sacraments.

The Elder Tobias

A second very instructive example of complete abandonment to the Divine Will in the midst of the greatest sufferings is furnished by the elder Tobias. Considered from a human point of view this great servant of God was certainly entitled to complete exemption from the painful trials which befell him; but far from it, we find that he was tried as gold and silver are tried in the fire.

From his earliest childhood he observed all things according to the law of God. When his countrymen fell into idolatry and worshipped false gods, he refused to join them, adoring at the prescribed times in the temple of Jerusalem, and faithfully offering his first fruits and tithes. Every third year he gave all his first fruits and tithes to the converts and strangers. The son that was born to him he taught from his infancy to fear God and to abstain from all sin.

The first of the many painful trials to which it pleased God to subject him, consisted in his being led away captive to Babylon with the rest of his people. Though perfectly innocent of the sins for which his nation was punished, he was made to share their chastisement as though he too had been a transgressor of the law. Did this misfortune make him lose his trust in God? Did it make him murmur against Divine Justice and forsake the way of virtue? Far from it. During the days of his captivity "he forsook not the way of truth. But every day he gave all he could get to his brethren, his fellow captives. He fed the hungry, and gave clothes to the naked, and he was careful to bury the dead and them that were slain." So devoted was he to this work of charity that when it was announced to him one day as he sat at table that a man had been slain in the street, he left his meal unfinished to go and bury the dead man. When he could no longer do this charitable work openly on account of a royal prohibition, he carried the dead secretly to his house by day and buried them by night.

Humanly speaking, should we not expect that for so great a charity Tobias should be exempted from further afflictions and rewarded with all kinds of temporal blessings? But observe how God treated him and put his virtue to a still severer test. One day when Tobias had come home, greatly fatigued from the work of burying the dead, and was resting in front of his house, hot dung from a swallow's nest fell upon his eyes and rendered him blind. Surely a most grievous misfortune – one calculated to shake the constancy of a man less virtuous. But he stood this additional test in a most edifying manner. Sacred Scripture says of him: "Now this trial therefore the Lord permitted to happen to him that an example might be given to posterity of his patience, as also of holy Job. For whereas he had always feared God from his infancy and kept his commandments, he repined not against God because the evil of blindness had befallen him, but continued immovable in the fear of God, giving thanks to God all the days of his life. For as the kings insulted over holy Job, so his relatives and kinsmen mocked at his life, saying: Where is thy hope for which thou gavest alms and buriedst the dead? But Tobias rebuked them, saying: Speak not so; for we are the children of the saints, and look for that life which God will give to those who never change their faith from Him."

Here was solid virtue indeed. Nor did God leave his faithful servant without his reward even in this life. Sometime afterwards he was cured of his blindness in a miraculous manner by the Archangel Raphael, who then said to him: "Because thou was acceptable to God, it was necessary that temptation (i.e., sufferings) should prove thee."

In this saintly man, we also have a beautiful example of perfect resignation to God in times of public chastisements. When one day his wife upbraided him and said to him: "It is evident that thy hope is come to nothing, and thy alms now appear," he sighed and began to pray with tears: "Thou art just, O Lord, and thy judgments are just, and all Thy ways mercy, and truth, and judgment. And now, O Lord, think of me, and take not revenge of my sins; neither remember my offenses, nor those of my parents. For we have not obeyed Thy commandments; therefore we are delivered to spoil, and to captivity, and to death, and are made a fable and a reproach to all nations amongst which Thou hast scattered us. And now, O Lord, great are Thy judgments, because we have not done according to Thy precepts, and have not walked before Thee."

In the same spirit of faith he exhorted his unfortunate countrymen to trust in God and to accept their afflictions in the spirit of humility and penance. "Thou art great, O Lord, forever, and Thy kingdom is unto all ages. For Thou scourgest and Thou savest; Thou leadest down to hell and Thou bringest up again; and there is none that can escape Thy hand. Give glory to the Lord, ye children of Israel, and praise Him in the sight of the Gentiles; because He hath therefore scattered you among the Gentiles who know Him not, that you may declare His wonderful works and make them know that there is no other almighty God besides Him. He hath chastised us for our iniquities, and He will save us for His own mercy. See then, what He hath done with us, and with fear and trembling give ye glory to Him, and extol the eternal King of glory in your works. As for me, I will praise Him in the land of my captivity, because He hath shown His majesty toward a sinful nation. Be converted, therefore, ye sinners, and do justice before God, believing that He will show His mercy to you. And I and my soul will rejoice with Him."

Surely an instructive example to confirm what has been said in these pages about the necessity of suffering for making the servants of God grow solid in virtue and to enable them to reach the highest degrees of sanctity here and of glory hereafter.

Saint Lidwina

A third example of perfect resignation and heroic patience under stress of prolonged suffering is St. Lidwina. This saint was born in a little town of Holland in the year 1380. In her youth she was possessed of great beauty, on which account she was eagerly sought in marriage by several young men. But she, enlightened by grace, spurned the world with its false pleasure and resolved to dedicate herself exclusively to the service of God by embracing a life of virginity. That her natural beauty might not prove a danger to her virtue, she begged of God to deprive her of it. Her prayer was heard.

In her fifteenth year while out skating one day in company with several companions, she fell on the rough ice in such a manner as to break a rib in her right side. This marked the beginning of a long train of sufferings which were to last without interruption for no less than thirty-eight years. An abscess formed in her side which defied the skill of the best physicians, and in the course of time became the source of an infection which spread over her body.

For some years she was able to move about, though only with considerable difficulty and pain; but the last thirty-three years of her life she was completely bedridden. Her sufferings increased as time went on. Gangrene appeared in the wound in her side and continued to spread. It was the source of intense pain, especially during the last seventeen years of her life, for she was no longer able to move any part of her body except her head and one arm.

Nor was this the extent of her sufferings. Besides the pains caused by sickness, she had to endure the bitter pangs of great poverty, especially during the winter season. Moreover, she suffered greatly from calumny, false suspicion, and harsh treatment at the hands of those who considered her an impostor.

While in the beginning she experienced considerable difficulty in perfectly resigning herself to the Divine Will, she soon learned to suffer with the most perfect disposition when at the advice of her confessor she made the bitter Passion and Death of Our Savior the constant subject of her meditation and received Holy Communion as often as her condition permitted. These two means enabled her to endure the pains of her long illness not only in a most patient manner but also with a wonderful joy and gladness.

After having thus been a victim of undeserved sufferings for the long space of thirty-eight years – from the age of fifteen to fifty-three – she died a happy and peaceful death in 1433. On March 14, 1890, Pope Leo XIII put the official sanction upon the veneration which had been given her by the faithful since the time of her death.

Saint John of the Cross

Another illustrious example of painful suffering cheerfully endured for the love of God is furnished us by St. John, surnamed of the Cross.

This saint was a contemporary of St. Teresa. Having resolved from his earliest childhood to live entirely for God, he devoted himself for some time to the care of the sick in hospitals, where, full of the spirit of charity, he faithfully performed the most menial services. Later on he entered the order of the Carmelites and was ordained a priest. Consumed by an ardent desire to attain the highest degrees of perfection in the love of God, he began to live a life of great austerity and severe penance. To keep the love of suffering always before his eyes, he adopted the name of John of the Cross. From this time forward his conduct was modeled after the words of St. Paul: "They that are Christ's have crucified their flesh with its vices and concupiscenses," and, "The world is crucified to me and I to the world."

Our saint's great thirst for suffering was fully satiated. Having, with the help of St. Teresa, undertaken the reform of the Carmelite order and the restoration of primitive observance, he encountered the most bitter opposition and was for a long time subjected to heartless persecution by those of the order who resented his attempt at renovation. Things went so far that they laid violent hands on him and held him captive for nine months in a very small and stifling cell, where he was tormented with continual insults and reproaches and denied the privilege of saying Mass.

But these sufferings, great as they were, served only to whet his appetite for still greater ones. When one day Our Lord appeared to him and said: "John, what reward dost thou ask for all that thou hast suffered for me?" the saint made this generous and heroic answer: "O Lord, I ask no other reward than to suffer and to be despised for Thy sake." What great love for the cross is revealed in this petition!

That he was sincere in this desire to suffer, is further proved by his conduct towards the end of his life. When, on account of his broken health, his superiors granted him permission to select any house of the order in which to pass his last days, he deliberately chose the one which was governed by a superior who had been his personal enemy, and from whom he could on that account expect but little sympathy and kindness. It turned out as was to be foreseen. For a considerable length of time he was made to feel keenly the resentment of this superior; and it was only when his unalterable patience and charity toward his persecutors convinced even his enemies that he was a great saint, that the persecution ceased and he was honored and revered as he deserved to be.

He died in 1591, in the forty-ninth year of his age, and was canonized December 27, 1726.

Thus did this saint love and cherish the cross, fully convinced that nothing aids us more in acquiring a perfect resemblance to Jesus Christ than sufferings and humiliations endured out of love for Him.

St. John the Baptist

In this saint we have a convincing proof of the truth that God employs sufferings for the purpose of raising His servants to the highest degree of sanctity, and for this reason often allows full liberty to the wicked to ill-treat and persecute them, even as He allowed full liberty to the Jews to ill-treat and persecute His Divine Son and cruelly put Him to death on the cross.

That St. John ranks among the highest of the saints is clear from the testimony of Our Lord in his regard. "Among them that are born of women there is not a greater than John the Baptist." It is just this circumstance that makes the story of his martyrdom an undeniable proof of what has been explained in these pages, namely, that the most exalted degrees of holiness here and of glory hereafter are attained only by means of great suffering.

The Gospel relates that John was taken prisoner at the command of Herod, because he had fearlessly reproved that wicked king for his sins of adultery and incest. In this way the saint was made to share the lot of most of the prophets, who were persecuted simply because they faithfully discharged the duties imposed on them by God of reproving men for their sins and crimes.

But should we not expect that in this case at least God would interfere and liberate St. John from the hands of his enemies, even as He afterwards liberated St. Peter in a miraculous manner, and this all the more because he was a near relative of Our Lord? But nothing of the kind happened. While St. John was lingering in prison, Our Lord was performing all kinds of miracles, healing the sick, giving sight to the blind, hearing to the deaf, and even restoring the dead to life. But He did nothing whatever to set his dearly beloved relative at liberty and save him from the cruel death that awaited him.

And what was the conduct of the saint while detained in prison? Did he repine, complain or murmur against the will of God? Did he wonder why the Savior seemed to be so utterly indifferent in his regard? Did he send messengers to Him to plead with Him for his release? He did none of these things. We read indeed that he sent some of his disciples to Christ; but it was not for the purpose of having them beg for his deliverance. He understood perfectly well that conformity to the Divine Will in all things, and the endurance of persecution for justice' sake, were essential for the attainment of the glory God had prepared for him.

Consider, in the next place, under what revolting circumstances he was put to death. The incestuous Herod gives a splendid banquet to his household and nobles. The daughter of the infamous Herodias dances before the guests as they sit at table. Herod conceives an impure love for her, and promises with an oath that he will give her whatsoever she will ask of him. But she, instructed by her wicked mother, begs for nothing less than the head of John to be brought to the banquet hall in a dish. The king is saddened by this request; but fearing those who had heard him make an oath bound promise, he commands the prophet to be beheaded.

Thus it came to pass that at the request of an impious woman, through a rash promise made at the suggestion of impure love, and in the midst of a riotous banquet, the greatest of all the prophets was mercilessly put to death, and his bleeding head carried into the banquet hall, to be viewed by the assembled guests. Can a more inhuman and revolting spectacle be imagined? But even this was not enough to satisfy the revenge of the immoral Herodias. It is related that she took the bleeding head and pierced it with needles, in this cruel way expressing the feelings of hatred she entertained for him who had so fearlessly reproved her for her wicked life.

In the meantime, Our Lord, Who knew perfectly well what was going on in the royal palace, did nothing whatever to hinder the execution of His sainted relative. He could with ease have rescued him from his impending martyrdom; He could have struck the executioner dead; He could have saved him in a thousand ways. But He allowed the infamous crime to be perpetrated.

And why all this? Because, in addition to his marvelous holiness, St. John needed a martyr's sufferings and death in order to merit that particular kind and degree of glory to which he had been predestined. Were it not for his persecution and martyrdom, he would now be occupying a much lower rank in Heaven than the one to which he has been elevated both for his sanctity and his martyrdom.

The Blessed Virgin Mary

If there ever was a saint who was entitled to the privilege of perfect freedom from every form of suffering it was Mary Immaculate, the glorious Mother of the eternal Son of God. How should the universal law of suffering apply to her, since by a most singular favor she was perfectly free from the least taint of sin? Not only was she immaculate in her conception, but she was so enriched with the choicest graces of God that she possessed a greater amount of these heavenly treasures in the beginning of her earthly life than the rest of the saints taken together possess at the end of theirs. Surely, no pain, no grief, no sorrow in any shape or form must ever approach this Immaculate Virgin.

But how different are the thoughts of God from the thoughts of men! We abhor suffering with our whole being, and think we are the favorites of God when we have nothing to give us pain; while God scatters sufferings lavishly among those whom He loves and calls His friends. In fact, the more He loves them, the more does He make them suffer. Hence He ordained that she who of all His creatures was the most beloved, should also be made to endure the greatest sorrows that a human heart can endure. It was her destiny to become the Queen of Martyrs as well as to be the Mother of God. Her sorrow was to be as boundless and vast as the broad expanse of the ocean.

Let us briefly consider what great sorrows God prepared for her and with what dispositions she accepted and bore them. See her in the temple of Jerusalem offering her Divine Child according to the prescriptions of the law. Holy Simeon, full of joy that he has at last seen the Light of the world, takes Him into his arms, and then address to Mary these prophetic words: "This Child is set for the fall and the resurrection of many in Israel, and for a sign which shall be contradicted. And thy own soul a sword shall pierce." How strange! Mary had just offered up the most perfect and most pleasing sacrifice that had ever been offered in that temple, and as a sign that God is pleased with her offering, He gives her to understand that for thirty-three years a cruel sword shall rankle in her breast, which shall not be withdrawn until the day of her Son's resurrection from the dead.

But how did she receive this painful prediction of lifelong sorrow? With the most perfect resignation to the adorable will of God. As the year before she gave a willing consent to the joyful message conveyed to her by the angel, so now she gives her willing consent to the message of grief and sorrow delivered to her by holy Simeon: "Behold the handmaid of the Lord; be it done unto me according to thy word."

What imagination can picture the extent and depth of Mary's sufferings from that day on until they ended on the morning when Christ rose gloriously from the tomb? That sword which during all those years pierced her heart was far sharper and more penetrating than earthly steel; for the latter can reach the body only; it cannot reach the soul. But of all the pains to which man is liable, those of the soul are the greatest and the hardest to bear. And such were for the most part those which Mary was made to endure.

Passing over the three and thirty years that she spent in the company of her Divine Son, during which time she had the vision of Calvary constantly before her eyes, let us briefly pass in review the sufferings she endured during the fearful hours that preceded His death on the cross. What inexpressible anguish must have wrung her loving heart at the news of her son's arrest, by which she fully understood that the prophecies concerning His passion were at last about to be accomplished. How oppressed she was with grief when she saw all the injuries, outrages and torments which His enemies inflicted on Him in the different stages of His passion. Her sorrow was in proportion to her love for her Son. But she loved Him not only as her child, but also as her God, with a love so perfect and so intense that it surpassed in an immeasurable degree the combined love of all the angels and saints in Heaven. Hence, the sufferings she endured during the lifetime of Our Lord, and especially during the hours of His passion, also surpassed in an immeasurable degree all the sufferings which the saints were called upon to endure for the sake of justice. So great was her anguish that but for a miraculous preservation of her life, she would have died of a broken heart long before her Son expired on the cross.

But what may have been the purpose of all this undeserved suffering? Why this excess of sorrow, of which she could truthfully say, "Great as the sea is my sorrow"? Why was Mary, this masterpiece of God's omnipotence, Virgin Immaculate and Mother of God, who surpassed all the angels in dignity and grace – why was she required to bear what was never required of the angels? The following reasons are perhaps the answer to the question:

Mary had received from God the singular privilege of the Immaculate Conception, enjoying perfect freedom from the least stain of sin and being enriched from the first moment of her existence with an inconceivable wealth of grace. For this she was to make a return of gratitude, which, though it could not be adequate, was to be as full as possible. She made the return largely by the sufferings she endured in union with her Divine son.

In addition to this, God conferred on her the still greater dignity of the Divine motherhood, a dignity unparalleled. For others might be created immaculate – as Adam and Eve actually were; but no one could share with her the glory of the Divine maternity. For this wonderful privilege she was to render to God the fullest measure of gratitude of which she was capable; and, as in the former case, sufferings were the coin in which a large part of her indebtedness was to be paid.

Besides being the Mother of God, she was also to be the Mother of the saints. It was. her special office to take a very intimate part in the redemption of sinners from the slavery of Satan, that they might become children of God, hence the place assigned to her at the foot of the cross. Hence, too, the title Co-Redemptrix, which the saints have applied to her. On Calvary, where she assisted her Divine Son in his last agony, she became our Mother in the order of grace. There she brought us forth unto the supernatural life amidst unspeakable agonies of pain. And as mothers usually have a very tender love for those children at whose birth they suffered greatly, so also does our heavenly Mother love us with a love that is second only to that which Jesus Christ bears us.

Lastly, Mary was destined to be the Queen of Heaven. She was to be placed over the whole of God's creation. As such she was to attain a degree of holiness that far surpassed the combined holiness of all the heavenly citizens. But how was she to attain it? How acquire the merits necessary for this singular exaltation? (For she was under the same law that we are under of meriting the glory of the next life.) By her perfectly faithful cooperation with every grace received during her life she merited for herself an exceedingly high degree of glory, it is true; so high, indeed, that if the glory of all the angels and saints were bestowed upon one person, it would bear no comparison with hers. But even this would fall short of what God had designed for her. How then was she to mount to those exalted heights to which God had decreed she should be elevated? There was one means by which she could accomplish this – it was suffering, lifelong and exceedingly bitter suffering.

This is the meaning of that ocean of sorrow into which her Immaculate Heart was plunged. This is the explanation of that sword which, according to Simeon's prophecy, was to remain fixed in her heart during the thirty-three years of her Son's life and was to torture her so unmercifully at the foot of the cross. Surely, a convincing proof of what we have tried to make plain in these pages, that sufferings play a necessary and important role in the lives of those whom God has predestined to the more exalted degrees of glory in Heaven.

Seventeen

Jesus Christ: The Man of Sorrows

In the first part of this work it was shown how sin is the one and only source of all the sufferings that afflict the children of men. Sin introduced all manner of physical and moral evils as a necessary result of the loss of our original perfection. Of ourselves we could do nothing whatever to improve our lot. We were miserable slaves of the worst of all tyrants, Satan, through whose envy sin was introduced into the world.

But God took pity on us. Moved by infinite compassion He sent His only begotten Son into the world to be its Savior and Redeemer. When the fullness of time had come, Jesus Christ appeared among men, being like to them in all respects, with the sole exception of sin. But He took on the appearance of a sinner, and in this guise presented Himself to His heavenly Father as a victim of reparation for the sins which we were indeed able to commit but not able to expiate.

But what a painful ordeal of suffering He underwent in order to make this reparation! Hear the plaintive cry that escapes His lips in the Garden of Olives: "Father, if it be possible, let this chalice pass from Me; but yet not My will, but Thine be done." His human nature, which like ours, was keenly sensitive to pain, shrank from the sufferings that awaited Him; but His intense love for us triumphed over the fear of pain and made Him go forth courageously to suffer and die that we might have life everlasting.

Think of this frequently, dear reader: Jesus Christ set such a high value on your immortal soul that He deliberately chose sufferings of the greatest intensity and endured them gladly that you might one day be admitted to the unspeakable bliss of His heavenly kingdom. Oh, how He yearned, all through His life, for the hour when He would consummate the sacrifice of His life for love of you! "I have a baptism wherewith I am to be baptized; and how am I straitened until it be accomplished!" He became a Man of Sorrows, that you might become a child of God.

The passion of Christ can be considered a new creation. But how different it was from the creation of the universe. The latter cost God no labor and no pain; but the former, the regeneration of man, what inconceivable labor and agonies of pain it cost the Son of God! Indeed so great was the suffering He endured for the sake of fallen man that we can speak of it only as the excess of the passion. Let us dwell on this point for a little while.

"From one point of view it might seem unnecessary for Our Lord to go to the extreme of suffering so much and dying; for His smallest action was of infinite merit, so that it exceeded all the demerits of the world, and could have purchased life for all. Yet there is a beautiful appropriateness and fitness in the excesses of the passion. The death of Christ is in accordance with that fundamental law, typified in all the ceremonies of the Old Testament, that without blood there is no remission. Throughout nature we trace the principle that death produces life. The spring is preceded by winter. The seed does not produce a new plant unless it first die. Life, then, must be preceded by an adequate death. Death is in reality, a vivifying action, a creative action, we may say; and is in itself the cure of death.

"The supernatural life of man, being a participation of the Infinite, must proceed from an infinite death. Our death in sin is irremediable as far as we are concerned, and in a manner infinite. It requires to be remedied by a death which is productive of God in us. Therefore God died in His human nature.

"The excess of Our Lord's passion is in full accordance with universal law. God destroys nothing; not even the energies of evil. He allows things to work out their activities to the full; He lets the battle rage till the evil exhausts itself and is broken like a wave on an iron bound coast. Sin, therefore, being in its tendency destructive of God, is allowed to go to its last extremity in destroying the life of God in human nature. Not till then had it done its worst; and after that it can do no further harm except what we deliberately invite upon ourselves. Our Lord rose again unharmed by it; and in that consists His victory. His triumph is thus far greater than if he had prevented sin; or stifled its energies by an extra legal intervention of new forces in the universe.

"In His passion Our Lord bore the whole brunt of all the sins of the world, and not merely those of His actual enemies. The hatred and fury of Caiphas, Pilate and Herod were the embodiment of our malice. But further, in Gethsemane He actually saw and endured the full horror of each individual sin that we have committed. How fearful would have been the consequences of our sins to us if they had not been exhausted on Our Lord? 'If in the green wood they do these things, what shall be done in the dry!'" (Bellord, *Meditations*.)

To conclude our reflections on the great subject of human suffering: Should not the attentive consideration of the excess of the sufferings of Jesus Christ help us to take a right view of the trials and afflictions that come into our life, and to bear them with perfect resignation for the love of Him, since by His bitter passion He has made it possible for us to sanctify every one of them and render them meritorious of the endless joys of Paradise?

Let us then know and understand: There is no other way to Heaven except the way of the cross. Well has the author of the Imitation of Christ said: "If there had been anything better and more profitable to man's salvation than suffering, then surely Christ would have shown it by word and example. For both the disciples that followed Him, and all who desire to follow Him, He plainly exhorteth to the bearing of the cross, and saith: 'If any one will come after Me, let him deny himself, take up his cross daily, and follow Me.' So that, when we have thoroughly read and searched all, let this be the final conclusion, that through much tribulation we must enter the kingdom of God."